Skills Scope and Sequence

The chart lists the following skill categories and skills (checked by week, Weeks 1–36):

Punctuation & Grammar
- Abbreviations
- Capital Letters
- Commas
- Language Usage
- Parts of Speech
- Possessive Nouns
- Quotation Marks
- Sentence Structure
- Sentence Types
- Singular/Plural Nouns
- Subject/Predicate

Comprehension
- Analogies
- Categorizing
- Cause & Effect
- Real & Make-Believe
- Sequencing

Vocabulary/Word Study
- Compound Words
- Consonant/Vowel Sounds
- Contractions
- Homophones
- Rhyme
- Synonyms/Antonyms
- Word Meaning from Context
- Word Family

Reference Skills
- Alphabetical Order
- Syllabication

Other Language Skills
- Correct/Incorrect Spelling
- Friendly Letter
- Identify the Mistake
- What Goes Here?

Week	Abbrev.	Capital Letters	Commas	Language Usage	Parts of Speech	Possessive Nouns	Quotation Marks	Sentence Structure	Sentence Types	Singular/Plural Nouns	Subject/Predicate	Analogies	Categorizing	Cause & Effect	Real & Make-Believe	Sequencing	Compound Words	Consonant/Vowel Sounds	Contractions	Homophones	Rhyme	Synonyms/Antonyms	Word Meaning from Context	Word Family	Alphabetical Order	Syllabication	Correct/Incorrect Spelling	Friendly Letter	Identify the Mistake	What Goes Here?
Week 1		X			X	X								X			X						X			X			X	
Week 2				X										X			X					X	X	X		X			X	
Week 3			X			X							X	X			X	X				X	X			X			X	
Week 4				X										X			X	X					X	X		X			X	
Week 5	X				X									X		X	X					X				X			X	
Week 6			X			X							X	X			X	X				X	X			X			X	
Week 7					X										X		X	X		X		X				X			X	
Week 8	X			X										X		X	X					X	X			X	X			X
Week 9	X			X										X		X				X		X					X	X		
Week 10			X								X		X	X			X	X				X	X			X			X	X
Week 11			X		X					X	X			X		X	X					X	X			X	X	X		
Week 12			X	X				X	X				X	X			X						X	X		X	X			
Week 13	X		X					X			X		X	X			X						X			X		X	X	
Week 14				X				X				X		X		X	X						X			X	X	X	X	
Week 15			X	X				X					X	X			X	X	X				X	X		X	X			
Week 16	X								X	X				X			X				X				X			X		
Week 17			X					X		X	X		X	X		X	X	X		X		X	X			X			X	
Week 18	X			X				X	X				X	X		X	X	X				X	X		X			X		
Week 19	X			X			X	X	X	X	X		X				X				X		X	X			X	X		
Week 20			X				X		X	X			X				X				X		X	X	X		X	X		
Week 21				X				X	X								X				X	X	X			X	X	X		
Week 22	X			X				X					X	X			X					X			X		X	X	X	
Week 23				X				X			X	X		X			X			X						X	X	X	X	
Week 24				X				X	X	X	X			X			X						X			X	X	X	X	
Week 25				X										X			X			X	X					X			X	
Week 26			X		X	X	X							X	X		X									X				X
Week 27	X			X				X	X					X			X			X		X	X			X			X	
Week 28	X		X					X						X			X									X			X	
Week 29			X	X	X			X	X					X			X	X		X	X		X			X		X		
Week 30	X			X				X						X			X			X			X			X			X	
Week 31			X					X					X				X	X	X	X	X	X	X			X			X	
Week 32	X		X		X	X		X	X					X			X									X	X	X		
Week 33	X		X	X	X			X						X			X				X		X			X	X		X	
Week 34	X				X	X	X	X	X			X					X			X			X					X	X	
Week 35				X	X			X					X	X			X			X						X	X			X
Week 36	X			X	X									X			X						X			X	X	X	X	X

©2005 Evan-Moor Corp. • Daily Language Review, Grade 2 • EMC 580

Sentence Editing Skills

Week	Correct Article	Double Negatives	Pronouns	Homophones	Plural Nouns	Run-on Sentences	Verb Forms	Contractions	Possessives	Words in a Series	Dates, Addresses	In Speech	End of Sentence	Period Abbreviations	Beginning of Sentence	Books, Titles of People	Other Proper Nouns
Week 1													×		×		×
Week 2	×				×								×		×		×
Week 3	×				×		×						×				×
Week 4	×				×	×		×	×				×		×	×	×
Week 5	×		×	×				×	×				×		×		×
Week 6	×				×	×			×				×				×
Week 7	×				×			×		×			×	×	×	×	×
Week 8	×				×		×	×	×				×		×		×
Week 9	×		×		×			×	×	×			×		×		×
Week 10	×				×								×	×	×	×	×
Week 11	×				×				×	×	×		×	×	×		×
Week 12	×		×	×					×	×			×	×	×		×
Week 13	×				×		×	×	×	×			×	×	×		×
Week 14	×		×	×		×			×				×	×	×		×
Week 15	×		×	×	×		×	×					×		×		×
Week 16	×							×	×				×	×	×		×
Week 17	×			×	×	×			×	×	×		×	×	×	×	×
Week 18	×		×	×	×	×		×	×	×	×		×	×	×		×
Week 19	×				×		×		×				×	×	×		×
Week 20	×				×	×		×	×				×	×	×		×
Week 21	×		×	×	×		×	×		×			×		×		×
Week 22	×		×	×			×	×	×	×	×		×	×	×	×	×
Week 23	×				×			×		×	×		×		×		×
Week 24	×		×	×				×	×	×	×		×	×	×	×	×
Week 25	×		×	×			×	×					×	×	×		×
Week 26	×				×	×		×			×		×				×
Week 27	×	×	×		×		×						×				×
Week 28	×				×			×	×				×				×
Week 29	×		×		×			×	×		×		×	×	×	×	×
Week 30	×		×	×				×	×	×			×	×			×
Week 31	×		×	×		×		×	×		×		×				×
Week 32	×		×	×	×				×	×			×	×	×	×	×
Week 33	×	×						×	×				×	×	×		×
Week 34	×	×		×		×	×	×	×		×		×				×
Week 35	×	×						×	×			×	×				×
Week 36	×	×	×						×			×	×				×

Daily Language Review, Grade 2 • EMC 580 • ©2005 Evan-Moor Corp.

Name: _____

Monday △ 1

Correct the sentences.

1. do you like to paint

_____

2. bob wants a pet dog

_____

Which words have the same sound as /a/ in "came"?

3. bag   train   make   stand

Find the words that rhyme.

4. do   to   so

5. hen   fan   pen

Name: _____

Tuesday △ 1

Correct the sentences.

1. willie swam in the pond

_____

2. will you feed the cat

_____

Which words have the same sound as /i/ in "him"?

3. pin   mine   sick

Is this a sentence?

4. ran down the street   yes   no

Which word is spelled correctly?

5. com   come   kome

Name:

Wednesday

Correct the sentences.

1. how fast did you run

_____

2. put your toys away

_____

Which words have the same sound as /u/ in "cup"?

3. fun   put   son

Which letter comes first in the alphabet?

4. o   e   i

Find the word that names something (noun).

5. funny   puppy   running

©2005 Evan-Moor Corp. • Daily Language Review, Grade 2 • EMC 580

Name:

Thursday

Correct the sentences.

1. are you going to the party

_____

2. did she fix the wagon

_____

Which letters can make the same sound?

3. c   k   m   ck

Which word is spelled correctly?

4. thu   the   dhe

Find the words that go together.

5. puppy   cat   shark   hamster

©2005 Evan-Moor Corp. • Daily Language Review, Grade 2 • EMC 580

Name:

Friday  1

Find the missing words.

1. We _____ going to the zoo.
        is   are

2. Sid _____ singing a song.
        is   are

3. We _____ go now.
      isn't   can't

4. That _____ my bike.
      don't   isn't

5. Mrs. Brown _____ a pie for dinner.
       made   make

Daily Progress Record 1

How many did you get correct each day? Color the squares.

	Monday	Tuesday	Wednesday	Thursday	Friday
5					
4					
3					
2					
1					

Monday 2

Correct the sentences.

1. anna and tonya are friends

_____

2. can carlos ride a bike

_____

Which words have the same sound as /e/ in "me"?

3. see   been   key   funny

Find the action words (verbs).

4. run   fly   happy   swim

Is this a statement or a question?

5. What time is it _____

Tuesday 2

Correct the sentences.

1. did them go on the class trip

_____

2. Mom and me ate ice cream

_____

Which words have the same sound as /i/ in "mine"?

3. skip   my   kite   I

Which go together?

4. robin   parrot   plane   owl

5. orange   corn   apple   banana

©2005 Evan-Moor Corp. • Daily Language Review, Grade 2 • EMC 580

Wednesday  2

Correct the sentences.

1. is that kim's parakeet

_____

2. look out for that car

_____

Name two words that are part of the -ay family.

3. _____

Which word is spelled correctly?

4. get   git   geet

Which letters are in alphabetical order?

5. f d e   j k l   a c b

©2005 Evan-Moor Corp. • Daily Language Review, Grade 2 • EMC 580

Thursday 2

Correct the sentences.

1. how many pigs was in the pen

_____

2. the sun were hot

_____

Which words mean the same?

3. small   fast   little   long

What word goes on the line?

4. Mother is going to town. _____ must go to the dentist.

Write two words that rhyme with "all."

5. _____

©2005 Evan-Moor Corp. • Daily Language Review, Grade 2 • EMC 580

Name:

Friday

©2005 Evan-Moor Corp. • Daily Language Review, Grade 2 • EMC 580

Find the missing words.

1. She _____ singing a song.
   was   were

2. His dogs _____ playing with a ball.
   was   were

3. Don't you _____ roller skates?
   got   have

4. Mark _____ up all the balloons.
   blue   blew

5. Ann went _____ in the lake.
   swims   swimming

Daily Progress Record

©2005 Evan-Moor Corp. • Daily Language Review, Grade 2 • EMC 580

How many did you get correct each day? Color the squares.

	Monday	Tuesday	Wednesday	Thursday	Friday
5					
4					
3					
2					
1					

Monday  3

Correct the sentences.

1. will you help sammy with his homework

_____

2. his bike is blue with a orange seat

_____

Tell the word that means more than one box.

3. _____

What two words are in "cupcake"?

4. _____

Put these letters in alphabetical order.

5. t v x u z w y _____

©2005 Evan-Moor Corp. • Daily Language Review, Grade 2 • EMC 580

Tuesday 3

Correct the sentences.

1. good for you

_____

2. will you mop that spill milk

_____

Which word is spelled correctly?

3. kup   cupe   cup

Number the words in alphabetical order.

4. ☐ bed   ☐ car   ☐ ant

Which words go together?

5. ten   six   many   twenty

©2005 Evan-Moor Corp. • Daily Language Review, Grade 2 • EMC 580

Wednesday  3

Correct the sentences.

1. them girls like to ride horses

_____

2. which toys is in the toy box

_____

Which word has the sound of /a/ in "bake"?

3. can   eight   wall   plant

What does "pokey" mean in this sentence?

4. The turtle was so pokey he came in last in the race.
    a. fast   b. slow   c. cute

Find the two words that rhyme.

5. me   been   three   time

©2005 Evan-Moor Corp. • Daily Language Review, Grade 2 • EMC 580

Thursday 3

Correct the sentences.

1. him and i are best friends

_____

2. what time will school been out

_____

Find the word that is the opposite of "soft."

3. fluffy   smooth   hard

Which word has the sound of /th/ in "three"?

4. then   thin   than

Write a make-believe sentence about a frog.

5. _____

©2005 Evan-Moor Corp. • Daily Language Review, Grade 2 • EMC 580

Friday

©2005 Evan-Moor Corp. • Daily Language Review, Grade 2 • EMC 580

Find the missing words.

1. Waldo went to the soccer game with _____.

     them   they   those

2. _____ have a funny bulldog for a pet.

    Them   They   Those

3. I _____ tie my shoe.

       cant   can't   cann't

4. Angela _____ be able to come with us.

        wasn't   wont   won't

5. Did you go to the _____ on your vacation?

          see   sea   seen

Daily Progress Record

©2005 Evan-Moor Corp. • Daily Language Review, Grade 2 • EMC 580

How many did you get correct each day? Color the squares.

	Monday	Tuesday	Wednesday	Thursday	Friday
5					
4					
3					
2					
1					

Monday ⚠4

©2005 Evan-Moor Corp. • Daily Language Review, Grade 2 • EMC 580

Correct the sentences.

1. where is they going

_____

2. dad and me are going to build a birdhouse

_____

Which word has the sound of /s/ in "see"?

3. his   mess   runs

Ask a question about snakes.

4. _____

Give the missing word.

5. girl : woman :: boy : _____

Tuesday ⚠4

©2005 Evan-Moor Corp. • Daily Language Review, Grade 2 • EMC 580

Correct the sentences.

1. mothers sewing box is in the den

_____

2. did he fixed the broken car

_____

Number the words in alphabetical order.

3. ☐down   ☐up   ☐in   ☐out

Find the word that is spelled correctly.

4. toof   tuth   tooth

Why were the children happy?

5. The children began to laugh when they saw it was snowing.

Wednesday

Correct the sentences.

1. <u>little red riding hood</u> is my sisters favorite book

_____

2. didnt it rain last sunday

_____

Find the words that tell about the dragon.

3. The huge green dragon scared the princess.

Which words go together?

4. cake   presents   monkeys   candles

Name two words in the -ish family.

5. _____

©2005 Evan-Moor Corp. • Daily Language Review, Grade 2 • EMC 580

Thursday

Correct the sentences.

1. he doesnt have no sisters

_____

2. why did they ran down the street

_____

Find the words that rhyme.

3. A fat cat sat on Dad's hat.

Is it a question or a statement?

4. did you like the pizza _____

Which word is spelled correctly?

5. cloce   close   cloose

©2005 Evan-Moor Corp. • Daily Language Review, Grade 2 • EMC 580

Name: _____

Friday 4

Find the missing word.

1. That dog _____ at me.

               bark   barked   barking

2. Pablo won _____ race.

               his   he   him

3. The class will take lunch with _____.

               they   them   there

4. I _____ to clean my room.

               has   gots   have

5. Mr. Smith _____, "Thank you for helping."

               say   saying   said

Daily Progress Record 4

How many did you get correct each day? Color the squares.

	Monday	Tuesday	Wednesday	Thursday	Friday
5					
4					
3					
2					
1					

Monday /5

Correct the sentences.

1. dads tools are in that box

   _____

2. is jerry the tall boy in the whole class

   _____

Which words have the same sound as /oo/ in "book"?

3. shook   tool   foot   hook

Is this a statement or a question?

4. Today is Ben's birthday _____

What word is missing?

5. sock : foot :: mitten : _____

©2005 Evan-Moor Corp. • Daily Language Review, Grade 2 • EMC 580

Tuesday /5

Correct the sentences.

1. does your baby sister crying a lot

   _____

2. the bear ate for big fish

   _____

What will happen next?

3. The telephone began to ring.
   a. I will open the door.   b. I will talk on the telephone.
   c. I will take the cake out of the oven.

Number the words in alphabetical order.

4. ☐ elephant   ☐ goose   ☐ deer

Which word is spelled correctly?

5. thoos   those   thoz

©2005 Evan-Moor Corp. • Daily Language Review, Grade 2 • EMC 580

Wednesday /5

Correct the sentences.

1. will you came to my house

_____

2. i brush my tooth every day

_____

Circle the words that tell about a bear.

3. big   strong   blue   furry

Which words have the sound of /o/ in "go"?

4. goat   so   drop   bone

Find the words that go together.

5. fork   spoon   knife   hammer

Thursday /5

Correct the sentences.

1. did you see that bird ate a worm

_____

2. mark cant find his homework

_____

Do these words rhyme?

3. her   fur   stir   yes   no

Write a question about a dinosaur.

4. _____

What is the correct way to spell **?**

5. wale   whale   well

Name: _____

Friday

©2005 Evan-Moor Corp. • Daily Language Review, Grade 2 • EMC 580

Find the missing words.

1. Mother _____ to the baby.
   sing   sang

2. Milk _____ everywhere when the carton broke.
   flied   flew

3. I had _____ apple for lunch.
   an   a

4. Put _____ boxes over there.
   them   those

5. They _____ get to go to the lake.
   can't   didn't

Daily Progress Record

How many did you get correct each day? Color the squares.

	Monday	Tuesday	Wednesday	Thursday	Friday
5					
4					
3					
2					
1					

©2005 Evan-Moor Corp. • Daily Language Review, Grade 2 • EMC 580

Name: _____

Monday 6

Correct the sentences.

1. the clown have a funny smile

_____

2. how fast can you runned

_____

Which words mean more than one of something?

3. cherry   rabbits   berries

What two words make this compound word?

4. cowgirl _____

Which word comes first in alphabetical order?

5. lion   butterfly   elephant   monkey

Name: _____

Tuesday 6

Correct the sentences.

1. susan can ride shes bike

_____

2. its in the brown sack

_____

Name two words in the -ill family.

3. _____

Which word is spelled correctly?

4. kar   car   carr

Find the sentence.

5. under the tree   Tom and Jose are   put the toys away

Wednesday

Correct the sentences.

1. when is youre birthday

   _____

2. i seen a big elephant at the zoo

   _____

Find the words that have the same beginning sound.

3. gum   giant   garden

Does the word "running"...?

4. a. name something   b. tell what it looks like   c. tell what it does

Find the words that rhyme.

5. king   wing   sang   ring

Thursday

Correct the sentences.

1. an aunt crawled up my arm

   _____

2. did you sea eggs in the nest

   _____

Find the word that is the opposite of "cold."

3. wet   hat   dark   hot

Find the words that end with the sound of /e/ in "me."

4. my   funny   silly   fly   pretty

Is it real or make-believe?

5. The butterfly sang a funny song.   _____

Friday

Find the missing words.

1. _____ help you wash the car.
        Ill   I'll

2. _____ too late to go now.
       It's   Its

3. Are you _____ have pizza for dinner?
       gonna   going to

4. Maggie and _____ are in the same class at school.
       I   me

5. The horse _____ over a tall wall.
       jump   jumped

Daily Language Review

Daily Progress Record

How many did you get correct each day? Color the squares.

	Monday	Tuesday	Wednesday	Thursday	Friday
5					
4					
3					
2					
1					

Name: _____

Monday

©2005 Evan-Moor Corp. • Daily Language Review, Grade 2 • EMC 580

Correct the sentences.

1. look out four that car

_____

2. my pet cat are small

_____

Find the words with the sound of /ar/ in "car."

3. star   hard   stay   dark

Which word is spelled correctly?

4. sed   sede   said   caid

What does "can't" mean?

5. cant not   could not   cannot

Name: _____

Tuesday

©2005 Evan-Moor Corp. • Daily Language Review, Grade 2 • EMC 580

Correct the sentences.

1. a toy jet am in the box

_____

2. mrs larson picked up the baby

_____

Which sound is the same in "paint" and "way"?

3. _____

Find the words that name (nouns).

4. box   jar   jump   Max

Is it real or make-believe?

5. Tanisha was in a hurry to get to the party. _____

Wednesday

Correct the sentences.

1. i had butter jelly and bread for a snack

   _____

2. that cake were yummy

   _____

Find the words that go together.

3. snow   stream   rain   wind

Add "ed" to these words.

4. play _____   want _____

Name two words in the -ow family.

5. _____

Thursday

Correct the sentences.

1. what did bobs puppy do

   _____

2. sam losted his hat

   _____

Find the two words that mean the same.

3. yell   tell   shout

Which words have the sound of /aw/ in "saw"?

4. paw   watch   came   tall

What does "isn't" mean?

5. _____

©2005 Evan-Moor Corp. • Daily Language Review, Grade 2 • EMC 580

©2005 Evan-Moor Corp. • Daily Language Review, Grade 2 • EMC 580

Name:

Friday

Find the missing words.

1. That _____ my backpack.

       isn't can't don't

2. Tony _____ find his lost jacket.

       isn't can't don't

3. Mr. and Mrs. Lee _____ want to go.

       isn't can't don't

4. Where _____ you going?

       is   are

5. My grandmother _____ on the roller coaster with me.

       rode   rided

Daily Progress Record

How many did you get correct each day? Color the squares.

	Monday	Tuesday	Wednesday	Thursday	Friday
5					
4					
3					
2					
1					

Monday

Correct the sentences.

1. dad and me were at home

_____

2. her pet cats collar broke

_____

Put "gold" and "fish" together to make a compound word.

3. _____

Which word is spelled correctly?

4. aks   ask   aske

Number the words in alphabetical order.

5. ☐ jump   ☐ run   ☐ hop   ☐ skip

©2005 Evan-Moor Corp. • Daily Language Review, Grade 2 • EMC 580

Tuesday

Correct the sentences.

1. was those hens laying eggs

_____

2. he wasnt at home today

_____

Find the words that rhyme.

3. fast   just   last

Find the missing words.

4. We _____ a picnic last Sunday.
       have   had   having

What is the abbreviation for "doctor"?

5. Mr.   Dr.   Capt

©2005 Evan-Moor Corp. • Daily Language Review, Grade 2 • EMC 580

Wednesday

Correct the sentences.

1. did uncle ted make an campfire

_____

2. lets go cook them fish

_____

Find the words with the sound of /th/ in "the."

3. then   there   this   three

What word is missing?

4. paw : dog :: fin : _____

Is it real or make-believe?

5. The spoon ran away from home.   _____

©2005 Evan-Moor Corp. • Daily Language Review, Grade 2 • EMC 580

Thursday

Correct the sentences.

1. wow, what a great present

_____

2. pablo didnt won his race

_____

Find the words that need capital letters.

3. texas   ann   puppy   monday

Name two words in the -ake family.

4. _____

Find the words that mean only one of something.

5. egg   toys   kitten   sun

©2005 Evan-Moor Corp. • Daily Language Review, Grade 2 • EMC 580

Name: _____

Friday

Find the missing words.

1. Jamal likes to _____ big books.
   red   read

2. Did you _____ the football game?
   see   sea

3. Don't let that _____ sting you!
   be   bee

4. _____ you going to bed now?
   Ain't   Aren't

5. The cars were _____ around the track.
   race   raced   racing

Daily Progress Record

How many did you get correct each day? Color the squares.

	Monday	Tuesday	Wednesday	Thursday	Friday
5					
4					
3					
2					
1					

Monday

Correct the sentences.

1. sandy and me is jumping rope

_____

2. did teds dog have four puppys

_____

Find the abbreviation for "Mister."

3. Mrs.   Mr.   Dr.

Which word is spelled correctly?

4. smil   smile   smille

What word is missing?

5. That is _____ skateboard.

   Marks   Mark's   Mark

Tuesday

Correct the sentences.

1. i went to the park with amy sally and maria

_____

2. mom want brad to baby-sit on friday

_____

Find the words that go together.

3. soccer   baseball   dance   football

What word is missing?

4. A frog _____ up and down.

   hop   hops   hopping

5. An _____ was in the candy jar.

        ant   aunt

©2005 Evan-Moor Corp. • Daily Language Review, Grade 2 • EMC 580

Name:

Wednesday

Correct the sentences.

1. is carys birthday on monday

_____

2. does miyeko live on elm street

_____

Find the words with the sound of /g/ in "giant."

3. germ   gobble   giraffe   girl

What word is the opposite of "long"?

4. _____

What will happen next?

5. The man's car has a flat tire.
   a. He will buy a new car.   b. He will fix the tire.   c. He will kick the car.

©2005 Evan-Moor Corp. • Daily Language Review, Grade 2 • EMC 580

Name:

Thursday

Correct the sentences.

1. lets play in jamals backyard

_____

2. did you break Mothers vase

_____

Find the missing word.

3. Pick _____ jacket up off the floor.
   Mario   Marios   Mario's

Which word is spelled correctly?

4. jumpt   jumpd   jumped

Make a statement about a monkey.

5. _____

©2005 Evan-Moor Corp. • Daily Language Review, Grade 2 • EMC 580

Name:

Friday

Does a capital go here? Yes or No

1. <u>mrs.</u> <u>garcia</u> has three <u>children</u>.
     a   b   c

   a. _____ b. _____ c. _____

2. when <u>will</u> <u>jim</u> and <u>mark</u> be here?
         a   b   c

   a. _____ b. _____ c. _____

3. <u>her</u> <u>birthday</u> is <u>june</u> 16.
     a   b   c

   a. _____ b. _____ c. _____

Daily Progress Record

How many did you get correct each day? Color the squares.

	Monday	Tuesday	Wednesday	Thursday	Friday
5					
4					
3					
2					
1					

©2005 Evan-Moor Corp. • Daily Language Review, Grade 2 • EMC 580

Name:

Monday

Correct the sentences.

1. i seen the yellow kitten go under the house

_____

2. did max sat the box on the top step

_____

Find the correct spelling.

3. yoo   yu   you

What does the word "gnaw" mean in this sentence?

4. The hungry dog began to gnaw the bone to get bits of meat.
   a. chew on   b. play with   c. carry

Make a compound word with "corn" and "pop."

5. _____

Name:

Tuesday

Correct the sentences.

1. did fran bob and carlos make a boat

_____

2. mrs robin was looking for grass for his nest

_____

Find the word that means the same as "fast."

3. slow   run   quick

Which words have the sound of /oy/ in "boy"?

4. soil   toy   going   boil

Number these names in alphabetical order.

5. ☐ Carl   ☐ Brad   ☐ Amos   ☐ David

32

Wednesday

Correct the sentences.

1. are angie and tony move

_____

2. anna gived my sister and me her dollhouse

_____

Which words go together?

3. three   blue   nine   four

Is it real or make-believe?

4. Campers cook dinner over a campfire. _____

Find the words that rhyme.

5. slow   go   gone   row

Thursday

Correct the sentences.

1. does you have a pet hamster

_____

2. william and me like to play games

_____

Which word is spelled correctly?

3. miny   manee   many

Where do the commas go?

4. Birds can fly sing and make nests.

5. Today is July 2 1996.

Name: _____

Friday

Does a period go here? Yes or No

1. i have a dog _(a)_ his name _(b)_ is squeeky _(c)_

   a. _____   b. _____   c. _____

2. they ate_(a)_ hot dogs for lunch_(b)_ what did you eat_(c)_

   a. _____   b. _____   c. _____

3. can you help me_(a)_ i need to put this up_(b)_ on that high shelf_(c)_

   a. _____   b. _____   c. _____

©2005 Evan-Moor Corp. • Daily Language Review, Grade 2 • EMC 580

Daily Progress Record

How many did you get correct each day? Color the squares.

5				
4				
3				
2				
1				
Monday	**Tuesday**	**Wednesday**	**Thursday**	**Friday**

34

©2005 Evan-Moor Corp. • Daily Language Review, Grade 2 • EMC 580

Monday

Correct the sentences.

1. she give the book to jack

   _____

2. mrs smith rided a bus

   _____

Which word is spelled correctly?

3. little   litle   littel

Find the sentence.

4. To play ball.   Down the street.   The kitten went up a tree.

What caused the girl to get wet?

5. Jane got wet when it began to rain.

   _____

Tuesday

Correct the sentences.

1. my friend send a note to jim and i

   _____

2. next sunday she will going to the zoo

   _____

Find the words that have the sound /u/ makes in "use."

3. cute   mule   push   music

Find the nouns.

4. down   tree   grass   day   warm

Write two words that rhyme with "pest."

5. _____

Wednesday

Correct the sentences.

1. toby rided his bike down the rode

_____

2. bob ran in a race on may 6 1997

_____

Which word is spelled correctly?

3. gud   gode   good

Find the words that go together.

4. milk   water   bread   juice

Where does the comma go?

5. a. Salem Oregon,   b. Salem, Oregon   c. Salem, Oregon,

Thursday

Correct the sentences.

1. do cats rabbits and hamsters has soft fur

_____

2. dont touch that hot stove

_____

Which word means more than one child?

3. childs   childes   children

Number the words in alphabetical order.

4. ☐ egg   ☐ gum   ☐ fat   ☐ his

Which words have the same ending sound?

5. bench   reach   sock   ditch

Name:

Friday 11

Does a capital letter go here? Yes or No

1. dr. jones is my dentist.
   a   b   c

   a. _____   b. _____   c. _____

2. i live in orlando, florida.
   a   b   c

   a. _____   b. _____   c. _____

3. stan and ollie live on park street.
            a   b   c

   a. _____   b. _____   c. _____

Daily Progress Record 11

How many did you get correct each day? Color the squares.

	Monday	Tuesday	Wednesday	Thursday	Friday
5					
4					
3					
2					
1					

Name: _____

Monday

Correct the sentences.

1. they runned after the mices

_____

2. did she go to pet pals to get cat food

_____

Which words have the sound of /oo/ in "boot"?

3. food   soon   cook   tooth

Which words need a capital letter?

4. new york   disneyland   river   kansas

What compound word can you make with "ball" and "base"?

5. _____

©2005 Evan-Moor Corp. • Daily Language Review, Grade 2 • EMC 580

Name: _____

Tuesday

Correct the sentences.

1. marta lives in dallas texas

_____

2. why are you going to canada in june

_____

Which word is spelled correctly?

3. smal   smale   small

Which word needs 's?

4. races   Pedros bike   is not

Is it real or make-believe?

5. Mr. Chang had dinner with a giant. _____

©2005 Evan-Moor Corp. • Daily Language Review, Grade 2 • EMC 580

Wednesday  /12

Correct the sentences.

1. the two ladys went shopping in portland

_____

2. did mr king kept slipping on the ice

_____

Which word is spelled correctly?

3. eny   iny   any

Find the words that go together.

4. Christmas   Easter   Sunday   Halloween

What does "damp" mean in this sentence?

5. Kim's hair was damp after her shower.
   a. messy   b. clean   c. wet

Thursday /12

Correct the sentences.

1. ken isnt hear

_____

2. ill ask my mom if i can go

_____

What contraction do these words make?

3. did not _____

Find the verbs in this sentence.

4. Kelly ate a big banana and drank some cold milk.

Name two words in the -ook family.

5. _____

©2005 Evan-Moor Corp. • Daily Language Review, Grade 2 • EMC 580

Name: _____

Friday 12

Do you need a comma? Yes or No

1. Bill __(a)__ Sam __(b)__ and Annie like __(c)__ to play basketball.

   a. _____ b. _____ c. _____

2. Mr. __(a)__ Ramirez was born on July __(b)__ 4 __(c)__ 1962.

   a. _____ b. _____ c. _____

3. I swam __(a)__ and hiked __(b)__ when I was in Tucson __(c)__ Arizona.

   a. _____ b. _____ c. _____

Daily Progress Record 12

How many did you get correct each day? Color the squares.

	Monday	Tuesday	Wednesday	Thursday	Friday
5					
4					
3					
2					
1					

©2005 Evan-Moor Corp. • Daily Language Review, Grade 2 • EMC 580

Monday /13

Correct the sentences.

1. i cant go to anns party

_____

2. arthur and me dont like snakes

_____

Which word is spelled correctly?

3. house   howse   hoose

Which word means more than one goose?

4. gooses   goose   geese

Find the missing word.

5. What are _____ going to do in the school play?

them there they

Tuesday /13

Correct the sentences.

1. dr garcia lives in that green house

_____

2. tammy drinked her milk and eat a apple

_____

Which words have the sound of /c/ in "cent"?

3. city   candy   cereal   center

Number the words in alphabetical order.

4. ☐ ham   ☐ hug   ☐ his

What will happen next?

5. Jay fell down and cut his leg.
   a. He will get up and play some more.
   b. He will rub dirt in the cut.
   c. He will get someone to put a bandage on the cut.

Name: _____

Wednesday

Correct the sentences.

1. does dr clark work in denver

_____

2. pedro is on the same team as carla tina and lee

_____

Which greeting is correct—a., b., or c.?

3. a. Dear, Grandma　　　　b. Dear Grandma　　　　c. Dear Grandma,

What word is missing?

4. fish : scales :: bird : _____

Find the words that are opposites.

5. clean　　　　white　　　　soft　　　　dirty

Name: _____

Thursday

Correct the sentences.

1. what did them do for christmas

_____

2. are you going to a halloween party

_____

What abbreviation is used for a married woman?

3. Mr.　　　　Ms.　　　　Mrs.

Is this a statement or a question?

4. Can you tell me what time it is? _____

Find the missing word.

5. Is a turtle _____ than a snail?
　　　　slow　slower　slowest

42

Name:

Friday  13

Is this word spelled correctly? Yes or No

1. <u>Kan</u> you <u>com</u> to my house to <u>play</u>?
     a   b   c

   a. _____   b. _____   c. _____

2. He <u>aks</u> me <u>two</u> <u>his</u> party.
        a   b c

   a. _____   b. _____   c. _____

3. Will Mark <u>give</u> me a piece <u>uf</u> <u>dat</u> pizza?
                a   b c

   a. _____   b. _____   c. _____

Daily Progress Record 13

How many did you get correct each day? Color the squares.

	Monday	Tuesday	Wednesday	Thursday	Friday
5					
4					
3					
2					
1					

Monday 14

Correct the sentences.

1. was mr ruiz washing his car

_____

2. the dirty boy was took a bath

_____

Which words have the sound of /wa/ in "water"?

3. watch   waste   wall   warm

Which word is spelled correctly?

4. funy   funney   funny

Which letter closing is correct—a., b., or c.?

5. a. Your friend   b. Your, friend   c. Your friend,

Tuesday 14

Correct the sentences.

1. cindy just learnt how to stop her bike

_____

2. dont you have no cookys

_____

Which is correct—a., b., or c.?

3. a. june 16, 1996   b. June 16, 1996   c. June 16 1996

Find the sentence.

4. Betty and Sam.   Under the red blanket.   Six birds flew.

Find the adjectives in this sentence.

5. Lee's fat puppy ran across the tall green grass.

Wednesday

©2005 Evan-Moor Corp. • Daily Language Review, Grade 2 • EMC 580

Correct the sentences.

1. will you bee here by 6 oclock

_____

2. a women was make cakes for the sale

_____

Find the missing word.

3. He climbed _____ up the ladder.

    quick   quicker   quickly

Number the words in alphabetical order.

4. ☐ pet   ☐ pat   ☐ put   ☐ pot

Which word is spelled correctly?

5. wif   with   wiht

Thursday

©2005 Evan-Moor Corp. • Daily Language Review, Grade 2 • EMC 580

Correct the sentences.

1. there was a lot of mouses in the barn

_____

2. did zeke get that splinter out of his feet

_____

Name two words in the -all family.

3. _____

Find the words that go together.

4. pink   gray   fuzzy   tan

Put the sentences in the order they happen.

5. ☐ A big yellow flower bloomed.   ☐ The plant began to grow.
   ☐ Seely planted a seed.   ☐ Leaves grew on the stem.

Name:

Friday

Do you need an apostrophe? Yes or No

1. <u>Dont</u> put <u>Kellys</u> wet <u>shoes</u> on the bed.
   　　a　　　b　　　　　c

   a. _____ b. _____ c. _____

2. Why <u>isnt</u> <u>Roys</u> bike at <u>his</u> house?
   　　　a　　b　　　　　　c

   a. _____ b. _____ c. _____

3. <u>These</u> <u>arent</u> <u>Mikes</u> books.
   　　a　　　b　　　c

   a. _____ b. _____ c. _____

Daily Progress Record

How many did you get correct each day? Color the squares.

	Monday	Tuesday	Wednesday	Thursday	Friday
5					
4					
3					
2					
1					

46

©2005 Evan-Moor Corp. • Daily Language Review, Grade 2 • EMC 580

Monday  15

Correct the sentences.

1. alan have a pet geese in a cage

_____

2. them boys was running a

_____

Find the adjectives in this sente

3. A small gray cat sat on the

Number the words in alphabeti

4. ☐ flower   ☐ basket

What does "soil" mean in this se

5. Rita dug in the soil to make it _____ ___e planted the seeds.
   a. sandbox   b. dirt in the garden   c. to get dirty

[handwritten note:] already have 24 copies of wk 15, in Brenda's desk.

Tuesday 15

Correct the sentences.

1. she has went to get a book

_____

2. have they throwed the trash away

_____

Ask a question about the circus.

3. _____

Find the words that rhyme.

4. my   try   funny   why

What does "Dr." mean?

5. _____

Wednesday  15

©2005 Evan-Moor Corp. • Daily Language Review, Grade 2 • EMC 580

Correct the sentences.

1. i and jessie like hot dogs with cheese

_____

2. did he break peters glasses

_____

What compound word can you make with "bow" and "rain"?

3. _____

Find the words with the sound /or/ in "for."

4. four   store   move   door

Is it real or make-believe?

5. I saw an elf dancing in the garden. _____

Thursday 15

©2005 Evan-Moor Corp. • Daily Language Review, Grade 2 • EMC 580

Correct the sentences.

1. who one the swimming race

_____

2. dad put a angel on top of the christmas tree

_____

Which word is spelled correctly?

3. uway   awy   away

How do you spell more than one?

4. fox _____ dish _____

Find the two words that mean the same.

5. grin   frown   smile   wink

Name:

Friday  15

©2005 Evan-Moor Corp. • Daily Language Review, Grade 2 • EMC 580

What punctuation do you need?

1. Sam __(a)__ Mary __(b)__ and Tito made a sand castle __(c)__

   a. _____   b. _____   c. _____

2. He can __(a)__ t go until he cleans the rabbit __(b)__ s cage __(c)__

   a. _____   b. _____   c. _____

3. Do you like mustard on your hamburger__(a)__ I don__(b)__t__(c)__

   a. _____   b. _____   c. _____

Daily Progress Record 15

©2005 Evan-Moor Corp. • Daily Language Review, Grade 2 • EMC 580

How many did you get correct each day? Color the squares.

	Monday	Tuesday	Wednesday	Thursday	Friday
5					
4					
3					
2					
1					

Name:

Monday

Correct the sentences.

1. thats the biggest tree i ever seen

_____

2. did you see the butterfly sat on that flower

_____

Which words need capital letters?

3. april   sunday   fish   maine

Which one is correct—a., b., or c.?

4. a. Boise Idaho,   b. Boise, Idaho   c. Boise, Idaho,

What does "cottage" mean in this sentence?

5. The old woman lived in a little cottage in the middle of a garden.
   a. a castle   b. an apartment   c. a small house

Name:

Tuesday

Correct the sentences.

1. will you make cards for valentines day

_____

2. the teacher read <u>charlottes web</u> to the class in april

_____

Which word is spelled correctly?

3. gril   jirl   girl   gurl

Find the missing word.

4. My little sister is _____ years old.
                    to   too   two

Who is this sentence about?

5. Mrs. Chin made a birthday cake. _____

50

Wednesday

Correct the sentences.

1. latishas family had a kwanzaa party

_____

2. how many sheep was in the farmers barn

_____

Find the words that go together.

3. bee   snake   ant   grasshopper

What word is the opposite of "sad"?

4. _____

Write two words in the -oy family.

5. _____

Thursday

Correct the sentences.

1. angus went to sea dr conrad

_____

2. were going to mexico in may

_____

How many syllables do you hear in these words?

3. elephant _____   umbrella _____

What happened in this sentence?

4. The green sled went down the hill.

_____

Find the missing word.

5. in : out :: up : _____

Name:

Friday

Is it spelled correctly? Yes or No

1. My <u>dog</u> ran <u>uway</u> from <u>hom</u>.
      a   b   c

   a. _____   b. _____   c. _____

2. <u>Wat</u> do you <u>want</u> <u>two</u> have for a snack?
    a   b   c

   a. _____   b. _____   c. _____

3. Did <u>Muther</u> make <u>that</u> dress <u>four</u> you?
       a   b   c

   a. _____   b. _____   c. _____

Daily Progress Record

How many did you get correct each day? Color the squares.

	Monday	Tuesday	Wednesday	Thursday	Friday
5					
4					
3					
2					
1					

Monday

Correct the sentences.

1. did you ever read <u>peter pan</u>

_____

2. we dont have no pets at our house

_____

Find the word that is spelled correctly.

3. quik   kwick   quick

Which two words have the same meaning?

4. present   goat   horse   gift

What caused Tim to break his arm?

5. Tim fell out of the tree and broke his arm.

_____

Tuesday

Correct the sentences.

1. cindy weared a dress socks and shoes

_____

2. mrs carter told us a funny story

_____

Find the nouns in this sentence.

3. Harry put some oranges and grapes on the table.

Write two words in the -eep family.

4. _____   _____

Fill in the missing words.

5. Larry _____ up a _____ balloon.
       blue   blew   blue   blew

©2005 Evan-Moor Corp. • Daily Language Review, Grade 2 • EMC 580

Wednesday

Correct the sentences.

1. how did bernie done that

_____

2. keesha found for easter eggs at the park

_____

Which words have the sound of /c/ in "nice"?

3. mice   stick   race   cent

Give a statement about peanut butter.

4. _____

What will happen next?

5. The bus stopped in front of the school.
   a. Shoppers will get off the bus.
   b. The driver will ask for money.
   c. Children will get off the bus.

Thursday

Correct the sentences.

1. the ship sail on march 20 1998

_____

2. kyle steve and me fed peanuts to them elephants

_____

Which word is spelled correctly?

3. stopped   stoppt   stoped

Which address is correct—a., b., or c.?

4. a. 623 First Street   b. 623 First Street   c. 623 First, Street
      Medford Oregon   Medford, Oregon   Medford, Oregon

Number the words in alphabetical order.

5. ☐ wish   ☐ zoo   ☐ zebra   ☐ want

54

Name:

Friday

Correct the vacation list. Use capitalization and punctuation.

We are going to visit:

1. yosemite national park   ....

2. lake tahoe   ....

3. mount lassen   ....

4. portland oregon   ....

5. seattle washington   ....

©2005 Evan-Moor Corp. • Daily Language Review, Grade 2 • EMC 580

Daily Progress Record

How many did you get correct each day? Color the squares.

	Monday	Tuesday	Wednesday	Thursday	Friday
5					
4					
3					
2					
1					

©2005 Evan-Moor Corp. • Daily Language Review, Grade 2 • EMC 580

Name:

Monday

18

©2005 Evan-Moor Corp. • Daily Language Review, Grade 2 • EMC 580

Correct the sentences.

1. there arent no children on the bus

2. mitch and naomi was following a path to the lake

How do you spell more than one?

3. train _____ bench _____

What word is the opposite of "dry"?

4. _____

Fill in the missing pronouns.

5. Sam and Pete got a pizza. _____ ate all of _____.

Name:

Tuesday
18

©2005 Evan-Moor Corp. • Daily Language Review, Grade 2 • EMC 580

Correct the sentences.

1. they want to help mr smith paint his dogs house

2. dont you have no snack four after school

Which word is spelled correctly?

3. blac   blak   black   blake

What compound word can you make with "water" and "melon"?

4. _____

Put the sentences in order.

5. ☐Alex put the lid on the paint and washed the brushes.
   ☐He painted the gate yellow.
   ☐Alex got a can of yellow paint and a brush.
   ☐He went to the fence in the backyard.

Wednesday

Correct the sentences.

1. why is Father going to dallas texas, in november

_____

2. the note were in mothers purse

_____

Find the words that go together.

3. stars   moon   mountain   sun

Which words have two syllables?

4. blanket   chase   under   sing

What does the word "trunk" mean in this sentence?

5. Grandma packed her good dishes in a big trunk to take to her new house.

   a. a dishwasher   b. an elephant's nose   c. a big box for holding things

©2005 Evan-Moor Corp. • Daily Language Review, Grade 2 • EMC 580

Thursday

Correct the sentences.

1. can you count to ten in spanish for mary and i

_____

2. otto lost a teeth last friday

_____

Which words have the sound of /j/ in "jam"?

3. jump   giraffe   get   giant   jelly

Find the verbs in this sentence.

4. Arturo ran down the field, grabbed the ball, and threw it to Amos.

Which words need capital letters?

5. he is going to move to florida in august.

©2005 Evan-Moor Corp. • Daily Language Review, Grade 2 • EMC 580

Name:

Friday

©2005 Evan-Moor Corp. • Daily Language Review, Grade 2 • EMC 580

Correct the addresses.

mr daniel james

123 maple street

memphis tennessee 00001

_____

_____

_____

mary ann jenkins

18 york avenue

madera california 00002

_____

_____

_____

Daily Progress Record

©2005 Evan-Moor Corp. • Daily Language Review, Grade 2 • EMC 580

How many did you get correct each day? Color the squares.

	Monday	Tuesday	Wednesday	Thursday	Friday
5					
4					
3					
2					
1					

Monday  19

Correct the sentences.

1. dont do that

_____

2. can you spell your friends name

_____

Which words have the sound of /er/ in "her"?

3. fur   stir   here   faster

Fill in the missing pronouns.

4. Mom has a basket. _____ puts flowers in _____.

Where does the apostrophe go?

5. Davids jacket

©2005 Evan-Moor Corp. • Daily Language Review, Grade 2 • EMC 580

Tuesday 19

Correct the sentences.

1. tammys toy spider has ate legs

_____

2. he want to ride kevins horse

_____

Which word is spelled correctly?

3. dont   donn't   don't

Find the words that rhyme with "peep."

4. sleep   sweet   keep   street

Is it real or make-believe?

5. He blew out the candles on his cake. _____

©2005 Evan-Moor Corp. • Daily Language Review, Grade 2 • EMC 580

Wednesday

Correct the sentences.

1. elephants is big strong and smart

_____

2. whats mrs cohn planting in her garden

_____

What is the contraction for "would not"?

3. wouldnt   would'nt   wouldn't

Who is this sentence about?

4. The baseball player hit a home run.

_____

Find the word that means "big."

5. long   large   little

Thursday

Correct the sentences.

1. will you gimme a orange

_____

2. dad beginned to mow the lawn after supper on monday

_____

Put the capitals and punctuation in this greeting.

3. dear aunt erma

How do you spell the word that means more than one pony?

4. _____

Which word is spelled correctly?

5. poosh   puch   push

Name:

Friday

Correct the birthday list. Use correct capitalization and punctuation.

Happy Birthday to You

cory brown
_____

january 3 1989
_____

dr sullivan
_____

december 11 1962
_____

mrs ann tosci
_____

may 1 1984
_____

Daily Progress Record

How many did you get correct each day? Color the squares.

	Monday	Tuesday	Wednesday	Thursday	Friday
5					
4					
3					
2					
1					

©2005 Evan-Moor Corp. • Daily Language Review, Grade 2 • EMC 580

Name:

Monday

Correct the sentences.

1. why was they running down the street

_____

2. lana and scott doesnt like snakes

_____

Which word means more than one berry?

3. berrys   berries   berry

Find the word that is the opposite of "mean."

4. strong   terrible   kind

Write two words in the -ick family.

5. _____

Name:

Tuesday

Correct the sentences.

1. im taking the book <u>three billy goats gruff</u> to school

_____

2. when will them eggs in the birds nest hatch

_____

Which word is spelled correctly?

3. muther   mother   muver

Number the words in alphabetical order.

4. ☐ sing   ☐ sang   ☐ sung   ☐ song

Fill in the missing words.

5. _____ saw a _____ bug on the flower stem.

    We   Wee   we   wee

Name: _____

Wednesday  /20

Correct the sentences.

1. petes dad taked the car to get gas

_____

2. dan said he doesnt never get to go fishing

_____

Tell what happened in this sentence.

3. A dragon grabbed the princess and flew away.

_____

Find the words that go together.

4. car   bus   boat   truck

What does "soles" mean in this sentence?

5. The hair on the soles of a polar bear's feet keep it from slipping in the snow.
   a. bottom of a polar bear's shoes   b. top of a polar bear's feet
   c. bottom of a polar bear's feet

Name: _____

Thursday /20

Correct the sentences.

1. ellen singed a song for mr and mrs larsen

_____

2. butch and elmer wasnt at the football game

_____

How many syllables in these words?

3. train _____   cookie _____

Put capitals and punctuation in this closing.

4. your friend
   derek

What happened when the boy dropped the lighted match?

5. Some grass started to burn when he dropped the match.

_____

©2005 Evan-Moor Corp. • Daily Language Review, Grade 2 • EMC 580

Name:

Friday

Correct this shopping list. Use correct capitalization and punctuation.

Go to:

happy pet shop

millers drugstore

takatas food market

Buy:

six cans of cat food

toothpaste shampoo and soap

apples corn and potatoes

Daily Progress Record

How many did you get correct each day? Color the squares.

	Monday	Tuesday	Wednesday	Thursday	Friday
5					
4					
3					
2					
1					

Monday  21

Correct the sentences.

1. dont fall off the tree branch

_____

2. did you see ant beth putting a flower in the vase

_____

Which word is spelled correctly?

3. more   mor   moer

Which word comes first in alphabetical order?

4. bunny   camel   bagel   jet

Find the missing word.

5. We all _____ when the clown did his tricks.
        claps   clapping   clapped

Tuesday 21

Correct the sentences.

1. leave me alone

_____

2. will the ponys be here by may 13 1999

_____

What does the contraction "we're" mean?

3. were   we are   we will

Find the missing word.

4. How many _____ were at your party?
        child   childs   children

Which words are opposites?

5. after   between   before   inside

Wednesday 21

©2005 Evan-Moor Corp. • Daily Language Review, Grade 2 • EMC 580

Correct the sentences.

1. does a octopus have ate legs

_____

2. keesha she has went to camp

_____

Which word has the sound of /ed/ in "wanted"?

3. filled   missed   planted

Which word is an adjective—a., b., or c.?

4. a. doctor   b. dirty   c. digging

Which words go together?

5. bread   muffin   banana   pancake   shovel

Thursday 21

©2005 Evan-Moor Corp. • Daily Language Review, Grade 2 • EMC 580

Correct the sentences.

1. me an my mom ate at burger king

_____

2. when can him and i have a turn on the swing

_____

Is it a statement or a question?

3. is a gorilla large _____

Tell a word that names more than one watch.

4. _____

Which words name insects?

5. a. be   bee   b. ant   aunt

Name:

Friday  21

Correct the punctuation mistakes. Write the letter correctly.

Dear Uncle Fred.

   May I go fishing with you the next time you go.
I would like to catch two big fish?

            Love?
            Sammy

Daily Progress Record 21

How many did you get correct each day? Color the squares.

	Monday	Tuesday	Wednesday	Thursday	Friday
5					
4					
3					
2					
1					

Monday

22

Correct the sentences.

1. theres a cup of soup and a orange in my lunch

_____

2. will mrs williams roast a thanksgiving turkey

_____

Find the words that rhyme with "fly."

3. bunny   cry   flip   buy

What will Caitlin do next—a., b., or c.?

4. Caitlin wants to go to her friend's house after school.
   a. She will call her mother and ask if she can go.
   b. She will go to her friend's house and then call her mother.
   c. She will go to her friend's for a while and then go home.

Which word is missing?

5. The children _____ on a field trip.
                    gone   went   going

Tuesday

22

Correct the sentences.

1. mr tylers truck had too flat tires

_____

2. is zeke living in los angeles california

_____

Find the word that is spelled correctly.

3. runing   runying   running

Which word goes with these words?—shoe, slipper, sandal

4. sock   mitten   boot   hat

Which word is a verb—a., b., or c.?

5. a. crying   b. furry   c. us

Wednesday  22

Correct the sentences.

1. did the babys bottle fell to the floor

_____

2. dad taked us to visit Grandmothers ranch

_____

Which word is the opposite of "open"?

3. work   into   close   go

What is the predicate of this sentence—a or b?

4. <u>Bob and Sam</u> <u>want a pet dog</u>.

       a   b

Which word is an adjective—a, b, or c?

5. The fat, <u>old</u> dog <u>went</u> to <u>sleep</u>.

         a   b   c

Thursday 22

Correct the sentences.

1. couldnt the librarian find <u>happy birthday moon</u> for you

_____

2. we was gone in june july and august

_____

Which words have the sound of /s/ in "his"?

3. buzz   miss   wish   flies

Which word has three syllables—a., b., or c.?

4. a. butterfly   b. inside   c. jumped

What happened when the baseball hit the window?

5. a. the ball bounced   b. the ball cracked   c. the window broke

Name: _____

Friday

Correct the mistakes.

Deer Tim,

    Whin are you koming to sea me?
We kan sleep in a tent an have u
campfire. We kan go swiming. Com soon.

          Your friend,
          Max

_____

_____

_____

_____

_____

Daily Progress Record

How many did you get correct each day? Color the squares.

	Monday	Tuesday	Wednesday	Thursday	Friday
5					
4					
3					
2					
1					

Name: _____

Monday

©2005 Evan-Moor Corp. • Daily Language Review, Grade 2 • EMC 580

Correct the sentences.

1. when are you gonna visit your uncle in reno nevada

_____

2. did she remember two put sugar in dads coffee

_____

Which word is spelled correctly?

3. wat   whut   what   waht

Which word comes first in alphabetical order?

4. x-ray   zebra   very   will

Find the missing word.

5. The dog and cat were _____ for the ball.

hunt   hunting   hunted

Name: _____

Tuesday

©2005 Evan-Moor Corp. • Daily Language Review, Grade 2 • EMC 580

Correct the sentences.

1. snakes turtles and alligators all has scales

_____

2. he don't want to read <u>snow white</u>

_____

Which word needs an apostrophe?

3. Jacks   eats   miss

Which word rhymes with "good"?

4. road   stood   flood

What word names more than one foot?

5. _____

Wednesday  23

©2005 Evan-Moor Corp. • Daily Language Review, Grade 2 • EMC 580

Correct the sentences.

1. my friends carl and mavis has a new pet rabbit

_____

2. why werent they eating them cookies

_____

Which words have the sound of /g/ in "go"?

3. gum   giant   gorilla   wiggle   gem

Which sentence is a statement—a. or b.?

4. a. Are there any dinosaurs in the zoo
   b. I saw a dinosaur skeleton in a book

Find the compound word.

5. grandmother   father   uncle

Thursday 23

©2005 Evan-Moor Corp. • Daily Language Review, Grade 2 • EMC 580

Correct the sentences.

1. she red <u>ramona the pest</u> to jim and i

_____

2. we is going fishing saturday

_____

What is the missing word?

3. chick : bird :: tadpole : _____

Find the missing word.

4. He _____ the baseball.   catched   caught

What caused Mrs. Cole to scream?

5. Mrs. Cole screamed when a mouse ran across her foot.

Name:

Friday  23

©2005 Evan-Moor Corp. • Daily Language Review, Grade 2 • EMC 580

Correct the mistakes.

Dear Mrs Evans

    Thank you for the toy monkey? Is so
soft and cute Ill take it to bed with me

          Your friend
          Tonya

Daily Progress Record 23

How many did you get correct each day? Color the squares.

	Monday	Tuesday	Wednesday	Thursday	Friday
5					
4					
3					
2					
1					

©2005 Evan-Moor Corp. • Daily Language Review, Grade 2 • EMC 580

Monday

Correct the sentences.

1. my parents was married on june 20 1989

   _____

2. do we live on mars earth or pluto

   _____

Which word is spelled correctly?

3. drinck   grink   drink   dreenk

Find the missing word.

4. Can Mark and _____ have a slice of pie?

         me   us   I

Which word has the same meaning as "tale"?

5. song   talk   story   lie

Tuesday

Correct the sentences.

1. the roses in dr winns garden bloom in may

   _____

2. what was they doing in the backyard

   _____

Which words start with capital letters?

3. easter   birthday   thursday   sign   july

How many syllables are in the word "pumpkin"?

4. _____ syllables

What is the subject of the sentence—a or b?

5. <u>Amy</u> <u>fed the cat and dog</u>.
   a   b

74

Wednesday

Correct the sentences.

1. how big are walters foots

_____

2. open your umbrella before it begin to rain

_____

Name two words in the -own family.

3. _____

Which words are nouns?

4. sing   jelly   sweep   sheep

What will happen next?

5. Mother Hen sat on her eggs until the shells cracked.
    a. She threw away the shells.   b. Her chicks came out of the shells.
    c. She ate the shells.

Thursday

Correct the sentences.

1. dont play with that sharp knife

_____

2. leeza lost for tooths this year

_____

Find the word that is the opposite of "fat."

3. tall   short   warm   thin

Find the missing word.

4. Mr. Tosci _____ us how to play soccer.
      taught   teached   learned

What does "recipe" mean in this sentence?

5. Follow the recipe if you want to make tasty cookies.
    a. steps to follow when you play a game
    b. steps to follow when you open a box of cookies
    c. steps to follow when you bake

Name:

Friday

Correct the mistakes.

Dere Amy

   kan you comm to my house to spend the night.
You and I will have fun

       luv
       Molly

Daily Progress Record

How many did you get correct each day? Color the squares.

	Monday	Tuesday	Wednesday	Thursday	Friday
5					
4					
3					
2					
1					

Monday

Correct the sentences.

1. the farmer feeded his sheeps all winter

_____

2. when i grow up, im going to bee a doctor

_____

Which word is spelled correctly?

3. ar   our   owr   aur

Find the pronouns in this sentence.

4. We played a game with them in our backyard.

Write the contraction for "did not."

5. _____

©2005 Evan-Moor Corp. • Daily Language Review, Grade 2 • EMC 580

Tuesday

Correct the sentences.

1. was there aunts on the picnic table

_____

2. the carpenter builded a tall fence and paint it white

_____

Which word means the same as "start"?

3. stop   begin   hurry   part

What word means more than one woman?

4. _____

Where do commas go in this sentence?

5. You will need a hammer nails paint and a paintbrush.

©2005 Evan-Moor Corp. • Daily Language Review, Grade 2 • EMC 580

Name: _____

Wednesday  /25

Correct the sentences.

1. when did mr ruiz learned to fly a airplane

_____

2. Do you like <u>red riding hood</u> or <u>tom thumb</u>

_____

Give two words in the -end word family.

3. _____   _____

Find the missing word.

4. Bill's kite _____ into a tree.

               blue   blew

Which word comes first in alphabetical order?

5. egg   end   eat   eel

©2005 Evan-Moor Corp. • Daily Language Review, Grade 2 • EMC 580

Name: _____

Thursday /25

Correct the sentences.

1. him and me went riding monday morning

_____

2. whats the small white kittens name

_____

Find the missing word.

3. The children were _____ to go to the circus.

             begs begged begging

How many syllables are in these words?

4. something _____   Halloween _____

What happened when the rocks fell?

5. His car was dented when the rocks rolled down the hill.

©2005 Evan-Moor Corp. • Daily Language Review, Grade 2 • EMC 580

Friday  25

Find the missing words.

1. It _____ in his room.

     wasn't   won't   weren't

2. _____ on the table in my room.

     Its   It's   Isn't

3. She works in a bank over _____.

     where   they're   there

4. Jose ran home as _____ as he could.

     quickest   quicker   quickly

5. Speedy is the _____ dog at the dog show.

     smart   smarter   smartest

©2005 Evan-Moor Corp. • Daily Language Review, Grade 2 • EMC 580

Daily Language Review

Daily Progress Record 25

How many did you get correct each day? Color the squares.

	Monday	Tuesday	Wednesday	Thursday	Friday
5					
4					
3					
2					
1					

©2005 Evan-Moor Corp. • Daily Language Review, Grade 2 • EMC 580

Monday

Correct the sentences.

1. did you put the milk butter and eggs in the refrigerator

_____

2. do you want to ate a egg for breakfast

_____

What is the abbreviation for "foot"?

3. dr.   ft.   in.   mrs.

Find the word that is the opposite of "play."

4. sit   run   work   sleep

Which word is spelled correctly?

5. huntting   smiling   skiping

Tuesday

Correct the sentences.

1. them dirty socks stink

_____

2. why does sid got a bigger piece than i gots

_____

Make two compound words using these words.

some   bow   rain   thing

3. _____

Name two words in the -oat word family.

4. _____

Is it real or make-believe?

5. Some birds lay eggs in nests.

Wednesday  26

Correct the sentences.

1. jeff didnt do nothing bad

_____

2. we was laughing at stans jokes

_____

Find the missing word.

3. Who is the _____ boy in school?
   tall   taller   tallest

4. Is your sister _____ than you?
   old   older   oldest

Correct the address.

5. lara smith
   217 york road
   forest park iowa

Thursday 26

Correct the sentences.

1. werent that a scary movie

_____

2. didnt you went to the christmas play

_____

Find the verbs in this sentence.

3. The yellow bus drove down the street and stopped at the corner.

What pronoun could take the place of "Mike" in this sentence?

4. Mike rode the bus home.

Find the missing word.

5. The princess _____ for the ball.
   dress   dressing   dressed

Name: _____

Friday

26

Find the missing words.

1. Who can jump the _____ —Carlos, Ryan, or Lee?
high   higher   highest

2. Honey is _____ than salt.
sweet   sweeter   sweetest

3. Give _____ carrot and _____ apple to the sheep.
a   an   a   an

4. Did you _____ the race?
win   won   one

5. Scott _____ the contest last year.
win   won   one

©2005 Evan-Moor Corp. • Daily Language Review, Grade 2 • EMC 580

Daily Progress Record

26

How many did you get correct each day? Color the squares.

	Monday	Tuesday	Wednesday	Thursday	Friday
5					
4					
3					
2					
1					

©2005 Evan-Moor Corp. • Daily Language Review, Grade 2 • EMC 580

Monday

Correct the sentences.

1. what did that man asks she and annie

_____

2. did them boys swam in the lake

_____

Find the abbreviation for a day of the week.

3. Dec.   Tsp.   Mon.

What is the subject of this sentence—a or b?

4. <u>A hungry hawk</u> <u>swooped down to catch a mouse</u>.
      a   b

How many syllables are in this word?

5. grandmother _____

Tuesday

Correct the sentences.

1. roger is my friend we like to do the same things

_____

2. what kind of ice cream does her like best

_____

Find the missing word.

3. What was Mother _____ about?
               smile   smiled   smiling

What two words are in "buttercup"?

4. _____   _____

What happened when it started to rain?

5. Megan opened her umbrella when it started to rain.

Wednesday

27

Correct the sentences.

1. how do them cats catch mouse

_____

2. put a apple in the basket

_____

Find the missing word.

3. We have a _____ girl in our class.

                        new   knew

What does the word "nimble" mean in this sentence?

4. The nimble goat jumped up on the roof of the farmer's shed.

        a. in a hurry   b. quick with good balance   c. long-haired

Which word means the same as "make"?

5. find   buy   take   build   tear

©2005 Evan-Moor Corp. • Daily Language Review, Grade 2 • EMC 580

Thursday

27

Correct the sentences.

1. what are you gonna do this week

_____

2. them dogs rolled in an mud puddle

_____

Which word is spelled correctly?

3. wuz   took   skippt

Find the abbreviation for a month of the year.

4. Fri.   Dec.   Dr.   Sat.

Name two words that rhyme with "same."

5. _____

©2005 Evan-Moor Corp. • Daily Language Review, Grade 2 • EMC 580

Name: _____

Friday  27

Find the missing words.

1. Those two _____ bought cars from the same sales_____.
   man   men   man   men

2. _____ just learned to ride _____ bike.
   He   Him   he   his   him

3. Herman helped _____ make _____ bed.
   me   my   me   my

4. Why _____ you like to swim?
   don't   doesn't

5. She _____ have a brother.
   don't   doesn't

Daily Progress Record 27

How many did you get correct each day? Color the squares.

5					
4					
3					
2					
1					
	Monday	Tuesday	Wednesday	Thursday	Friday

Monday 28

Correct the sentences.

1. the rooster on Grandpas farm crow at sunrise

_____

2. tim didnt know the way to dr glenns office

_____

What word is missing?

3. green : color :: _____ : number

Find the missing word.

4. _____ baseball uniform is in the closet.
        Petes   Pete's

5. How much do your _____ eat in one day?
         rabbits   rabbit's

Tuesday 28

Correct the sentences.

1. luis and me pick some oranges in mr lees orchard

_____

2. do jamal and tanisha living on wilson street

_____

What punctuation mark is missing in this sentence—a., b., c., or d.?

3. Ruth James and Troy take singing lessons.
      a. ?   b. ,   c. .   d. nothing is missing

Find the missing word.

4. A herd of _____ ate grass in the meadow.
       moose   mooses   meese

What does "fare" mean in this sentence?

5. Sally paid her fare to the bus driver so she could ride to her job.
      a. a present given to the bus driver
      b. money given to the bus driver
      c. something nice said to someone

Wednesday  28

Correct the sentences.

1. ken and me likes to play in the snow

_____

2. them children skated across a icy pond

_____

"Fri." is the abbreviation for what word?

3. _____

Which words have three syllables—a., b., c., or d.?

4. a. playing   b. butterfly   c. Saturday   d. messy

What is the predicate of this sentence—a or b?

5. <u>The snowstorm</u> <u>lasted all day</u>.
     a   b

©2005 Evan-Moor Corp. • Daily Language Review, Grade 2 • EMC 580

Thursday 28

Correct the sentences.

1. dont put the birdcage on miss bells desk

_____

2. are you gonna wash the dirty dishes

_____

Find the missing words.

3. George shouted _____ than anyone else at the game.
           loud   louder   loudest

4. Six _____ were resting on the lake.
     goose   geese   gooses

Which words are verbs—a, b, or c?

5. They <u>sang</u> and <u>danced</u> all around the <u>room</u>.
     a   b   c

©2005 Evan-Moor Corp. • Daily Language Review, Grade 2 • EMC 580

Name: _____

Friday

Find the missing words.

1. I want _____ ice-cream cone with _____ cherry on top.
             a an   a an

2. _____ plane flew over my house.
          A An

3. Will you _____ supper at my house?
           eat eating ate

4. That blue bird _____ on the tree branch.
           land landed landing

5. Did he _____ across the lake?
      swam swum swim

Daily Progress Record

How many did you get correct each day? Color the squares.

	Monday	Tuesday	Wednesday	Thursday	Friday
5					
4					
3					
2					
1					

Monday

Correct the sentences.

1. sam and george were bestest friends

_____

2. saturday was so hot that us all went to the beach

_____

Which words have the same sound as the /ea/ in "dream"?

3. need   bead   bread   clean

Find the word that does <u>not</u> belong.

4. alligator   lion   tiger   bobcat

Which is correct?

5. My uncle joined the army on _____.
   a. July 26 1995   b. July, 26, 1995   c. July 26, 1995

Tuesday

Correct the sentences.

1. mr feinstein took sid david and mary to yellowstone park

_____

2. them hates pickles

_____

What is the correct abbreviation for "street"?

3. a. Str.   b. St.   c. ST

How do you write the word for more than one dish?

4. _____

Find the sentence.

5. a. Matt and Karen
   b. flew across the sky in a hot-air balloon
   c. Cats have whiskers

Name: _____

Wednesday  29

Correct the sentences.

1. little bo peep losted her sheeps

_____

2. a big black hairy spider scared miss muffet

_____

Which word does <u>not</u> belong?

3. soap   toothbrush   spoon   comb

Which contraction would the two words make?

4. do not _____

5. I will _____

©2005 Evan-Moor Corp. • Daily Language Review, Grade 2 • EMC 580

Name: _____

Thursday 29

Correct the sentences.

1. mother was buy shoes for my brother and i

_____

2. when can jimmy and me open them christmas presents

_____

What does the word "okra" mean?

3. Grandma made a tasty soup with peas, carrots, okra, and onions.

    a. a poisonous plant   b. beef bones   c. a kind of vegetable

Which word comes first in alphabetical order?

4. knot   into   ladder   jeep

Which words mean the same thing?

5. merry   happy   sick   sleepy   glad

©2005 Evan-Moor Corp. • Daily Language Review, Grade 2 • EMC 580

Name:

Friday

Find the missing words.

1. Two _____ ran across the backyard.

    fox   fox's   foxes

2. How many _____ are in the pen?

    goose   gooses   geese

3. _____ Adams took her children to see a play.

    Mr.   Mrs.   She

4. _____ like to play games.

    I   Me   Us

5. When is _____ birthday?

    our   your   mine

eview, Grade 2 • EMC 580

Daily Progress Record

How many did you get correct each day? Color the squares.

	Monday	Tuesday	Wednesday	Thursday	Friday
5					
4					
3					
2					
1					

Monday

Correct the sentences.

1. do they live on maple street or west road

_____

2. can you get to sharp pencils for me

_____

Which word is spelled correctly?

3. thay   sno   some   gud

What is the missing word?

4. ear : hear :: mouth : _____

Find the missing word.

5. This has been the _____ winter of all time.
             cold   colder   coldest

Tuesday

Correct the sentences.

1. today is may 18 1997

_____

2. did you read <u>dear mr henshaw</u>

_____

Find the missing word.

3. The Christmas tree _____ when the lights were turned on.
       sparkling   sparkled   sparkles

What word is spelled correctly?

4. becuz   tree   gril   git

Number the words in alphabetical order.

5. ☐ ball   ☐ book   ☐ bell   ☐ bird

Wednesday

Correct the sentences.

1. mrs garcias little girl was sick

_____

2. should she gone to see dr hill

_____

Write a word that is the opposite of "first."

3. _____

Write two words in the -ight word family.

4. _____   _____

Find the missing word.

5. She _____ lived here for six years.
              have   has   will

Thursday

Correct the sentences.

1. dont put that there in your mouth

_____

2. am i getting presents for mine birthday

_____

Find the missing word.

3. They _____ off the cliff into the sea.
         dives   diving   dived

What does "won't" mean?

4. _____

Circle the subject of this sentence.

5. A boy named Tony moved in next door to me.

Name:

Friday

©2005 Evan-Moor Corp. • Daily Language Review, Grade 2 • EMC 580

Find the missing words.

1. That dog _____ at me.
     bark   barked   barking

2. Pablo won _____ race.
          he   his   him

3. The class will take lunch with _____.
                          they   them   there

4. I _____ to clean my room.
        has   gots   have

5. Mr. Smith _____, "Thank you for helping."
          say   saying   said

Daily Progress Record

©2005 Evan-Moor Corp. • Daily Language Review, Grade 2 • EMC 580

How many did you get correct each day? Color the squares.

	Monday	Tuesday	Wednesday	Thursday	Friday
5					
4					
3					
2					
1					

Name:

Monday  31

Correct the sentences.

1. why did manuel runned up and down the stairs

_____

2. aunt rosa put chicken corn and cookies in a picnic basket

_____

Find the compound word.

3. question   jellyfish   shaker

What does "galloped" mean in this sentence?

4. The horse "galloped" around the track and won the race.

    a. walked along   b. rode in a truck   c. ran quickly

Which word is the opposite of "told"?

5. gave   now   asked   begged

©2005 Evan-Moor Corp. • Daily Language Review, Grade 2 • EMC 580

Name:

Tuesday 31

Correct the sentences.

1. hurray four our team

_____

2. marthas hamster runned around on its wheel

_____

Find the missing word.

3. Bill went to _____ a skateboard.

       by   buy

Which word comes first in alphabetical order?

4. rose   queen   orange   pretty

What caused the hole in the barn wall?

5. A mouse made a hole in the barn wall by chewing the wood.

_____

©2005 Evan-Moor Corp. • Daily Language Review, Grade 2 • EMC 580

Name: _____

Wednesday

Correct the sentences.

1. uncle max eat pancakes eggs and bacon every sunday

_____

2. clean up that mess right now

_____

Find the two words that rhyme.

3. fly   whale   tie   show

Fill in the missing word.

4. Mother _____ a package to Uncle Raul.
          ship shipped shipping

Which words are nouns?

5. I <u>gave</u> the clerk <u>money</u> for the <u>book</u>.
     a   b   c

Name: _____

Thursday

Correct the sentences.

1. yoshi didnt do none of his homework

_____

2. her pet rabbit had ate babys

_____

Which word has two syllables?

3. principal   story   cry

Fill in the missing word.

4. pilot : plane :: driver : _____

What does "I'm" mean?

5. _____

Friday /31\

Find the missing words.

1. Cut _____ orange in half and put it in _____ bowl.
            a   an   a   an

2. Mother was _____ the baby a bath.
                   give gives giving

3. They _____ wait for the game to start.
             can't cant canned

4. _____ rode _____ bike up the hill.
         He His Him   he him his

5. I was _____ up the spilled water.
         mops mopping mopped

Daily Progress Record /31\

How many did you get correct each day? Color the squares.

	Monday	Tuesday	Wednesday	Thursday	Friday
5					
4					
3					
2					
1					

Name:

Monday  32

©2005 Evan-Moor Corp. • Daily Language Review, Grade 2 • EMC 580

Correct the sentences.

1. him and her was taking the dog for a walk

2. why didnt you ate the mushrooms on your pizza

Find the adjectives in this sentence.

3. The happy girl won a shiny new bike in the big contest.

Find the missing words.

4. Amy wants _____ to come to _____ party.
                   we   us   she   her

Which words mean more than one?

5. tooth   feet   mice   woman

Name:

Tuesday 32

©2005 Evan-Moor Corp. • Daily Language Review, Grade 2 • EMC 580

Correct the sentences.

1. how many chickens do farmer taylor got

2. mr and mrs morris has for children

Find the nouns.

3. The helicopter landed in a field by my house.

Which words go together?

4. pond   lake   boat   ocean   fish

What does "messenger" mean in this sentence?

5. The messenger brought us a big box from Uncle Sergio.
   a. person who sends things
   b. person who brings things
   c. person who makes things

Name:

Wednesday

Correct the sentences.

1. my sister and me mowed the lawn on saturday

   _____

2. did some flys land on his pudding

   _____

Number the words in alphabetical order.

3. ☐ jelly   ☐ bread   ☐ butter   ☐ milk

Make two compound words using these words.

   in   to   apple   sauce   side   pine

4. _____   _____

Correct the greeting.

5. dear mr president _____

Name:

Thursday

Correct the sentences.

1. have you red a story about a geese that laid golden eggs

   _____

2. arnold and lisa gots mickey mouse watches

   _____

What pronouns go on each line?

3. Carlos has a rabbit. _____ feeds _____ carrots.

Which words have the same meaning?

4. look   hear   see   speak

Where do the quotation marks go?

5. What is your name? asked Anita.

Name: _____

Friday

What punctuation do you need?

1. <u>Im</u> helping <u>Mrs</u> <u>Chin</u>
     a   b   c

   a. _____ b. _____ c. _____

2. Why <u>cant</u> <u>Jeffs</u> sister come with <u>us</u>
          a   b   c

   a. _____ b. _____ c. _____

3. <u>Dads</u> tie has <u>black</u> white, and red dots on <u>it</u>
     a   b   c

   a. _____ b. _____ c. _____

Daily Progress Record

How many did you get correct each day? Color the squares.

	Monday	Tuesday	Wednesday	Thursday	Friday
5					
4					
3					
2					
1					

©2005 Evan-Moor Corp. • Daily Language Review, Grade 2 • EMC 580

Monday 33

Correct the sentences.

1. mr clark is a vet at the san diego zoo

_____

2. youd better hurry the school bus is coming

_____

Write two words in the -eat word family.

3. _____   _____

Find the missing word.

4. _____ play a game.

     Lets   Let   Let's

What word is missing?

5. story : read :: song : _____

Tuesday 33

Correct the sentences.

1. i have some cupcakes do you want one

_____

2. a old man sitted on the bench and eated an apple

_____

Which word is spelled correctly?

3. uway   over   miny

Which word is the opposite of "now"?

4. then   maybe   next   how

What causes the baby to laugh?

5. My baby sister always laughs when I make funny faces.

_____

Name:

Wednesday

Correct the sentences.

1. i cant play now can you come back later

_____

2. ringly brothers circus is coming to town on october 19

_____

Where do the quotation marks go in this sentence?

3. Annie said, I like chocolate ice cream.

What word means more than one peach?

4. _____

Find the missing word.

5. Do you _____ how to ice-skate?

        no   now   know

Name:

Thursday

Correct the sentences.

1. lets plant flowers by mrs olsons fence

_____

2. my room is a mess mom says i haves to clean it now

_____

Which word does <u>not</u> belong?

3. quack   meow   woof   jump   cheep

Number the words in alphabetical order.

4. ☐sheep ☐horse ☐goat ☐pig

Which word has one syllable?

5. inside   many   friend   family

Friday

/33

Does a capital letter go here? Yes or No

1. <u>dr</u>. Winston <u>lives</u> in <u>texas</u>.
   a   b   c

   a. _____   b. _____   c. _____

2. Today <u>is</u> <u>monday</u>, <u>june</u> 16.
       a   b   c

   a. _____   b. _____   c. _____

3. <u>alex</u> and <u>jake</u> are <u>twins</u>.
   a   b   c

   a. _____   b. _____   c. _____

Daily Progress Record

/33

How many did you get correct each day? Color the squares.

	Monday	Tuesday	Wednesday	Thursday	Friday
5					
4					
3					
2					
1					

Monday /34

©2005 Evan-Moor Corp. • Daily Language Review, Grade 2 • EMC 580

Correct the sentences.

1. do you wants to go swimming then put on your swimsuit

_____

2. dont leave no toys on the stairs

_____

Find the missing word.

3. The cook made a cake for _____ and _____ .

                                   he him his   I me my

How do you spell the word that means more than one child?

4. _____

Which is correct?

5. a. Your friend,   b. your, friend   c. your, friend,   d. none of these

---

Tuesday /34

©2005 Evan-Moor Corp. • Daily Language Review, Grade 2 • EMC 580

Correct the sentences.

1. my sister and me seen a octopus at marine world

_____

2. im ten years old how old are you

_____

Which words rhyme?

3. it   eight   say   late   meet

4. Tell a make-believe sentence about a flower.

_____

5. Tell something real about a flower.

Name:

Wednesday  34

Correct the sentences.

1. he eight a big slice of apple pie he drink some milk

_____

2. which puppy do you want i want the won with spots

_____

Find the verbs in this sentence.

3. The monkey ran up the tree, swung by its tail, and picked a banana.

What word is missing?

4. Ellen picked out the _____ pumpkin in the field.
   large   larger   largest

Correct the address.

5. 16 sunset avenue
   willow utah 78462

©2005 Evan-Moor Corp. • Daily Language Review, Grade 2 • EMC 580

Name:

Thursday 34

Correct the sentences.

1. we found an old tin horn a rag doll and a spinning top in grandmas trunk

_____

2. i cant tie my shoes will you help me

_____

Find the missing words.

3. The children are _____ a fort out of old _____.
   maked   makes   making   box   boxes   boxed

Where does the apostrophe go?

4. Marilyns horse   Joys hens

What does "flock" mean in the sentence?

5. The brave dog guarded the flock of sheep while they grazed on the hillside.
   a. lost animal   b. bunch of animals   c. farm animal

©2005 Evan-Moor Corp. • Daily Language Review, Grade 2 • EMC 580

Name:

Friday

©2005 Evan-Moor Corp. • Daily Language Review, Grade 2 • EMC 580

Is it spelled correctly? Yes or No

1. <u>Wil</u> you <u>plai</u> <u>with</u> me?
   a   b   c

   a. _____   b. _____   c. _____

2. Mike <u>kan't</u> <u>ride</u> <u>u</u> horse.
         a   b c

   a. _____   b. _____   c. _____

3. A kangaroo <u>wuz</u> <u>hopin</u> up and <u>down</u>.
            a   b   c

   a. _____   b. _____   c. _____

Daily Progress Record

©2005 Evan-Moor Corp. • Daily Language Review, Grade 2 • EMC 580

How many did you get correct each day? Color the squares.

	Monday	Tuesday	Wednesday	Thursday	Friday
5					
4					
3					
2					
1					

Monday

Correct the sentences.

1. dad said, did you done that

_____

2. what does you have for lunch i have a hot dog

_____

Which date is correct?

3. a. July, 4, 1776   b. july 4, 1776   c. July 4, 1776

Find the missing words.

4. Help _____ find _____ umbrella.
      her hers she   her hers she

What does the abbreviation "Mon." mean?

5. _____

Tuesday

Correct the sentences.

1. miss kincaid painted a picture of my dog and i

_____

2. lets have a party said maggie

_____

What word means more than one lady?

3. _____

Find the missing word.

4. His little brother was _____ his teddy bear.
              hug   hugging   hugged

Where do the quotation marks go?

5. Let's go get some ice cream, said David

Wednesday

Correct the sentences.

1. yokos new skateboard is blew and read

_____

2. raul falled of his bike he broke his arm

_____

Number the words in alphabetical order.

3. ☐ zoom   ☐ zebra   ☐ zipper

What word is missing?

4. rabbit : fast :: turtle : _____

Which words rhyme with "way"?

5. main   they   stay   take

Thursday

Correct the sentences.

1. where did you got that book can i read it

_____

2. dont climb up that old ladder it isnt safe

_____

Find the words with two syllables.

3. under   pickle   chair   boxes   whale

Where does an apostrophe go in these words?

4. wont _____   lets _____

Name one more thing in this category.

5. peas   carrots   beans   _____

Friday  35

Correct the letter.

june 12 1998

dear aunt beth

   we has a new puppy i named him whiskers
dont you think thats a gud name kan you come to
seen whiskers you will like him

         luv
         martina

©2005 Evan-Moor Corp. • Daily Language Review, Grade 2 • EMC 580

Daily Progress Record 35

How many did you get correct each day? Color the squares.

	Monday	Tuesday	Wednesday	Thursday	Friday
5					
4					
3					
2					
1					

©2005 Evan-Moor Corp. • Daily Language Review, Grade 2 • EMC 580

Monday

Correct the sentences.

1. please put your toys away, mom said.

   _____

2. my grandma lives in chicago we are gonna visit her

   _____

Find the compound words.

3. Did you see the butterfly sitting on that yellow sunflower?

Find the missing word.

4. He has _____ the books back to the library.

   took taking taken

5. Will you be _____ in the show?

   sing singed singing

Tuesday

Correct the sentences.

1. they come to see us on thursday they left on friday

   _____

2. lee said, lets get something to drink

   _____

Which words name people?

3. teacher parrot Mary doctor jeep

Which words are misspelled?

4. Did the <u>bear</u> pick <u>sum</u> berries <u>of</u> the <u>bush</u>?
         a   b   c   d

What is the subject of this sentence?

5. A bumpy toad jumped into the pond.

110

Wednesday

Correct the sentences.

1. did you brush your tooths and wash your foots

_____

2. when will dinner be ready she asked

_____

Find the missing word.

3. They have _____ my new parrot.

        saw seen seeing

Find the word that is spelled correctly.

4. frend   frende   friend

What does the word "coop" mean in this sentence?

5. Kristen puts her hens in their coop every night to keep them safe from harm.

    a. a dish for chicken feed   b. a kind of basket   c. a pen for chickens

---

Thursday

Correct the sentences.

1. i am in second grade, said tara

_____

2. will you go into town with me i dont like to go by myself

_____

Number the words in alphabetical order.

3. ☐ squirrel   ☐ skates   ☐ shoe   ☐ store

What is the subject of this sentence?

4. The hungry cows ate grass in the meadow.

What is the predicate of this sentence?

5. The teacher liked my story.

Name:

Friday

Correct the letter.

october 14 1998

dear charlie

will you come to me halloween party
we ar gonna wear costumes and plays games
my mom will cook gud things to eat

your friend
pedro

_____

_____

_____

_____

_____

Daily Progress Record

How many did you get correct each day? Color the squares.

	Monday	Tuesday	Wednesday	Thursday	Friday
5					
4					
3					
2					
1					

Answer Key

Monday
1. Do you like to paint?
2. Bob wants a pet dog.
3. train   make
4. do   to
5. hen   pen

Tuesday
1. Willie swam in the pond.
2. Will you feed the cat?
3. pin   sick
4. no
5. come

Wednesday
1. How fast did you run?
2. Put your toys away.
3. fun   son
4. e
5. puppy

Thursday
1. Are you going to the party?
2. Did she fix the wagon?
3. c   k   ck
4. the
5. puppy   cat   hamster

Friday
1. are
2. is
3. can't
4. isn't
5. made

Monday
1. Anna and Tonya are friends.
2. Can Carlos ride a bike?
3. see   key   funny
4. run   fly   swim
5. question

Tuesday
1. Did they go on the class trip?
2. Mom and I ate ice cream.
3. my   kite   I
4. robin   parrot   owl
5. orange   apple   banana

Wednesday
1. Is that Kim's parakeet?
2. Look out for that car!
3. Answers will vary.
4. get
5. j k l

Thursday
1. How many pigs were in the pen?
2. The sun was hot.
3. small   little
4. She
5. Answers will vary.

Friday
1. was
2. were
3. have
4. blew
5. swimming

Monday
1. Will you help Sammy with his homework?
2. His bike is blue with an orange seat.
3. boxes
4. cup   cake
5. t u v w x y z

Tuesday
1. Good for you!
2. Will you mop that spilled milk?
3. cup
4. ant   bed   car
5. ten   six   twenty

Wednesday
1. Those girls like to ride horses.
2. Which toys are in the toy box? OR
   Which toy is in the toy box?
3. eight
4. b. slow
5. me   three

Thursday
1. He and I are best friends.
2. What time will school be out?
3. hard
4. thin
5. Answers will vary.

Friday
1. them
2. They
3. can't
4. won't
5. sea

Monday
1. Where are they going?
2. Dad and I are going to build a birdhouse.
3. mess
4. Answers will vary, but must be questions.
5. man

Tuesday
1. Mother's sewing box is in the den.
2. Did he fix the broken car?
3. down   in   out   up
4. tooth
5. They saw it was snowing.

Wednesday
1. Little Red Riding Hood is my sister's favorite book.
2. Didn't it rain last Sunday?
3. huge   green
4. cake   presents   candles
5. Answers will vary.

Thursday
1. He doesn't have any sisters.
2. Why did they run down the street?
3. fat   cat   sat   hat
4. question
5. close

Friday
1. barked
2. his
3. them
4. have
5. said

Monday
1. Dad's tools are in that box.
2. Is Jerry the tallest boy in the whole class?
3. shook   foot   hook
4. statement
5. hand

Tuesday
1. Does your baby sister cry a lot?
2. The bear ate four big fish.
3. b. I will talk on the telephone.
4. deer   elephant   goose
5. those

Wednesday
1. Will you come to my house?
2. I brush my teeth every day.
3. big   strong   furry
4. goat   so   bone
5. fork   spoon   knife

Thursday
1. Did you see that bird eat a worm?
2. Mark can't find his homework.
3. yes
4. Answers will vary, but must be in question form.
5. whale

Friday
1. sang
2. flew
3. an
4. those
5. didn't

Monday
1. The clown has a funny smile.
2. How fast can you run?
3. rabbits   berries
4. cow   girl
5. butterfly

Tuesday
1. Susan can ride her bike.
2. It's in the brown sack.
3. Answers will vary.
4. car
5. Put the toys away.

Wednesday
1. When is your birthday?
2. I saw a big elephant at the zoo.
3. gum   garden
4. c. tell what it does
5. king   wing   ring

Thursday
1. An ant crawled up my arm.
2. Did you see eggs in the nest?
3. hot
4. funny   silly   pretty
5. make-believe

Friday
1. I'll
2. It's
3. going to
4. I
5. jumped

Monday

1. Look out for that car!
2. My pet cat is small. OR My pet cats are small.
3. star   hard   dark
4. said
5. cannot

Tuesday

1. A toy jet is in the box.
2. Mrs. Larson picked up the baby.
3. a
4. box   jar   Max
5. real

Wednesday

1. I had butter, jelly, and bread for a snack.
2. That cake was yummy.
3. snow   rain   wind
4. played   wanted
5. Answers will vary.

Thursday

1. What did Bob's puppy do?
2. Sam lost his hat.
3. yell   shout
4. paw   watch   tall
5. is not

Friday

1. isn't
2. can't
3. don't
4. are
5. rode

Monday

1. Dad and I were at home.
2. Her pet cat's collar broke.
3. goldfish
4. ask
5. hop   jump   run   skip

Tuesday

1. Were those hens laying eggs?
2. He wasn't at home today.
3. fast   last
4. had
5. Dr.

Wednesday

1. Did Uncle Ted make a campfire?
2. Let's go cook those fish.
3. then   there   this
4. fish
5. make-believe

Thursday

1. Wow, what a great present!
2. Pablo didn't win his race.
3. Texas   Ann   Monday
4. Answers will vary.
5. egg   kitten   sun

Friday

1. read
2. see
3. bee
4. Aren't
5. racing

Monday
1. Sandy and I are jumping rope.
2. Did Ted's dog have four puppies?
3. Mr.
4. smile
5. Mark's

Tuesday
1. I went to the park with Amy, Sally, and Maria.
2. Mom wants Brad to baby-sit on Friday.
3. soccer   baseball   football
4. hops
5. ant

Wednesday
1. Is Cary's birthday on Monday?
2. Does Miyeko live on Elm Street?
3. germ   giraffe
4. short
5. b. He will fix the tire.

Thursday
1. Let's play in Jamal's backyard.
2. Did you break Mother's vase?
3. Mario's
4. jumped
5. Answers will vary.

Friday
1. a. yes   b. yes   c. no
2. a. no   b. yes   c. yes
3. a. yes   b. no   c. yes

Monday
1. I saw the yellow kitten go under the house.
2. Did Max set the box on the top step?
3. you
4. a. chew on
5. popcorn

Tuesday
1. Did Fran, Bob, and Carlos make a boat?
2. Mrs. Robin was looking for grass for her nest.
3. quick
4. soil   toy   boil
5. Amos   Brad   Carlos   David

Wednesday
1. Are Angie and Tony moving?
2. Anna gave my sister and me her dollhouse.
3. three   nine   four
4. real
5. slow   go   row

Thursday
1. Do you have a pet hamster?
2. William and I like to play games.
3. many
4. Birds can fly, sing, and make nests.
5. Today is July 2, 1996.

Friday
1. a. yes   b. no   c. yes
2. a. no   b. yes   c. no
3. a. no   b. no   c. yes

Monday
1. She gave the book to Jack.
2. Mrs. Smith rode a bus.
3. little
4. The kitten went up a tree.
5. It began to rain.

Tuesday
1. My friend sent a note to Jim and me.
2. Next Sunday she will go to the zoo.
3. cute   mule   music
4. tree   grass   day
5. Answers will vary.

Wednesday
1. Toby rode his bike down the road.
2. Bob ran in a race on May 6, 1997.
3. good
4. milk   water   juice
5. b. Salem, Oregon

Thursday
1. Do cats, rabbits, and hamsters have soft fur?
2. Don't touch that hot stove!
3. children
4. egg   fat   gum   his
5. bench   reach   ditch

Friday
1. a. yes   b. yes   c. no
2. a. no   b. yes   c. yes
3. a. yes   b. no   c. yes

Monday
1. They ran after the mice.
2. Did she go to Pet Pals to get cat food?
3. food   soon   tooth
4. New York   Disneyland   Kansas
5. baseball

Tuesday
1. Marta lives in Dallas, Texas.
2. Why are you going to Canada in June?
3. small
4. Pedro's bike
5. make-believe

Wednesday
1. The two ladies went shopping in Portland.
2. Did Mr. King keep slipping on the ice?
3. any
4. Christmas   Easter   Halloween
5. c. wet

Thursday
1. Ken isn't here.
2. I'll ask my mom if I can go.
3. didn't
4. ate   drank
5. Answers will vary.

Friday
1. a. yes   b. yes   c. no
2. a. no   b. no   c. yes
3. a. no   b. no   c. yes

Monday
1. I can't go to Ann's party.
2. Arthur and I don't like snakes.
3. house
4. geese
5. they

Tuesday
1. Dr. Garcia lives in that green house.
2. Tammy drank her milk and ate an apple.
3. city   cereal   center
4. ham   his   hug
5. c. He will get someone to put a bandage on the cut.

Wednesday
1. Does Dr. Clark work in Denver?
2. Pedro is on the same team as Carla, Tina, and Lee.
3. c. Dear Grandma,
4. feathers
5. clean   dirty

Thursday
1. What did they do for Christmas?
2. Are you going to a Halloween party?
3. Mrs.
4. question
5. slower

Friday
1. a. no   b. no   c. yes
2. a. no   b. no   c. yes
3. a. yes   b. no   c. no

Monday
1. Was Mr. Ruiz washing his car?
2. The dirty boy was taking a bath.
3. watch   wall   warm
4. funny
5. c. Your friend,

Tuesday
1. Cindy just learned how to stop her bike.
2. Don't you have any cookies?
3. b. June 16, 1996
4. Six birds flew.
5. fat   tall   green

Wednesday
1. Will you be here by 6 o'clock?
2. A woman was making cakes for the sale.
3. quickly
4. pat   pet   pot   put
5. with

Thursday
1. There were a lot of mice in the barn.
2. Did Zeke get that splinter out of his foot?
3. Answers will vary.
4. pink   gray   tan
5. 4   2
   1   3

Friday
1. a. yes   b. yes   c. no
2. a. yes   b. yes   c. no
3. a. no   b. yes   c. yes

Monday
1. Alan has a pet goose in a cage.
2. Those boys were running after the ball.
3. small   gray   soft   blue
4. basket   bow   flower   ribbon
5. b. dirt in the garden

Tuesday
1. She has gone to get a book. OR
   She went to get a book.
2. Have they thrown the trash away?
3. Answers will vary, but must be in question form.
4. my   try   why
5. Doctor

Wednesday
1. Jessie and I like hot dogs with cheese.
2. Did he break Peter's glasses?
3. rainbow
4. four   store   door
5. make-believe

Thursday
1. Who won the swimming race?
2. Dad put an angel on top of the Christmas tree.
3. away
4. foxes   dishes
5. grin   smile

Friday
1. a. comma   b. comma   c. period
2. a. apostrophe   b. apostrophe   c. period
3. a. question mark   b. apostrophe   c. period

Monday
1. That's the biggest tree I ever saw. OR ...I have
   ever seen.
2. Did you see the butterfly sitting on that flower?
3. April   Sunday   Maine
4. b. Boise, Idaho
5. c. a small house

Tuesday
1. Will you make cards for Valentine's Day?
2. The teacher read Charlotte's Web to the class
   in April.
3. girl
4. two
5. Mrs. Chin

Wednesday
1. Latisha's family had a Kwanzaa party.
2. How many sheep were in the farmer's barn?
3. bee   ant   grasshopper
4. happy
5. Answers will vary.

Thursday
1. Angus went to see Dr. Conrad.
2. We're going to Mexico in May.
3. elephant _3_   umbrella _3_
4. went down the hill
5. down

Friday
1. a. yes   b. no   c. no
2. a. no   b. yes   c. no
3. a. no   b. yes   c. no

Monday
1. Did you ever read <u>Peter Pan</u>?
2. We don't have any pets at our house.
3. quick
4. present   gift
5. He fell out of the tree.

Tuesday
1. Cindy wore a dress, socks, and shoes.
2. Mrs. Carter told us a funny story.
3. Harry   oranges   grapes   table
4. Answers will vary.
5. blew   blue

Wednesday
1. How did Bernie do that?
2. Keesha found four Easter eggs at the park.
3. mice   stick   race   cent
4. Answers will vary, but must be a statement.
5. c. Children will get off the bus.

Thursday
1. The ship sailed on March 20, 1998. OR
   The ship will sail on March 20, 1998.
2. Kyle, Steve, and I fed peanuts to those elephants.
3. stopped
4. b. 623 First Street Medford, Oregon
5. want   wish   zebra   zoo

Friday
1. Yosemite National Park
2. Lake Tahoe
3. Mount Lassen
4. Portland, Oregon
5. Seattle, Washington

Week

Monday
1. There aren't any children on the bus.
2. Mitch and Naomi were following a path to the lake.
3. trains   benches
4. wet (moist, damp)
5. They   it

Tuesday
1. They want to help Mr. Smith paint his dog's house.
2. Don't you have a snack for after school?
3. black
4. watermelon
5. 4
   3
   1
   2

Wednesday
1. Why is Father going to Dallas, Texas, in November?
2. The note was in Mother's purse. OR The notes were…
3. stars   moon   sun
4. blanket   under
5. c. a big box for holding things

Thursday
1. Can you count to ten in Spanish for Mary
   and me?
2. Otto lost a tooth last Friday.
3. jump   giraffe   giant   jelly
4. ran   grabbed   threw
5. He   Florida   August

Friday

Mr. Daniel James
123 Maple Street
Memphis, Tennessee 00001

Mary Ann Jenkins
18 York Avenue
Madera, California 00002

Monday

1. Don't do that!
2. Can you spell your friend's name?
3. fur   stir   faster
4. She   it
5. David's jacket

Tuesday

1. Tammy's toy spider has eight legs.
2. He wants to ride Kevin's horse.
3. don't
4. sleep   keep
5. real

Wednesday

1. Elephants are big, strong, and smart.
2. What's Mrs. Cohn planting in her garden?
3. wouldn't
4. The baseball player
5. large

Thursday

1. Will you give me an orange?
2. Dad began to mow the lawn after supper on Monday.
3. Dear Aunt Erma,
4. ponies
5. push

Friday

Cory Brown
January 3, 1989

Dr. Sullivan
December 11, 1962

Mrs. Ann Tosci
May 1, 1984

Monday

1. Why were they running down the street?
2. Lana and Scott don't like snakes.
3. berries
4. kind
5. Answers will vary.

Tuesday

1. I'm taking the book <u>Three Billy Goats Gruff</u> to school.
2. When will those eggs in the bird's nest hatch? OR
   ...the birds' nest hatch?
3. mother
4. sang   sing   song   sung
5. We   wee

Wednesday

1. Pete's dad took the car to get gas.
2. Dan said he doesn't ever get to go fishing.
3. grabbed the princess and flew away
4. car   bus   truck
5. c. bottom of a polar bear's feet

Thursday

1. Ellen sang a song for Mr. and Mrs. Larsen.
2. Butch and Elmer weren't at the football game.
3. train <u>1</u>   cookie <u>2</u>
4. Your friend,
   Derek
5. Some grass started to burn.

Friday

Happy Pet Shop	six cans of cat food
Miller's Drugstore	toothpaste, shampoo, and soap
Takata's Food Market	apples, corn, and potatoes

Monday
1. Don't fall off the tree branch!
2. Did you see Aunt Beth putting a flower in the vase?
3. more
4. bagel
5. clapped

Tuesday
1. Leave me alone!
2. Will the ponies be here by May 13, 1999?
3. we are
4. children
5. after   before

Wednesday
1. Does an octopus have eight legs?
2. Keesha has gone to camp. OR
   Keesha went to camp.
3. planted
4. b. dirty
5. bread   muffin   pancake

Thursday
1. My mom and I ate at Burger King.
2. When can he and I have a turn on the swing?
3. question
4. watches
5. a. bee
   b. ant

Friday
Dear Uncle Fred,

   May I go fishing with you the next time you go?
I would like to catch two big fish.

         Love,
         Sammy

Monday
1. There's a cup of soup and an orange in my lunch.
2. Will Mrs. Williams roast a Thanksgiving turkey?
3. cry   buy
4. a. She will call her mother and ask if she can go.
5. went

Tuesday
1. Mr. Tyler's truck had two flat tires.
2. Is Zeke living in Los Angeles, California?
3. running
4. boot
5. a. crying

Wednesday
1. Did the baby's bottle fall to the floor?
2. Dad took us to visit Grandmother's ranch.
3. close
4. b
5. a

Thursday
1. Couldn't the librarian find <u>Happy Birthday, Moon</u>
   for you?
2. We were gone in June, July, and August.
3. buzz   flies
4. a. butterfly
5. c. the window broke

Friday
Dear Tim,

   When are you coming to see me?
We can sleep in a tent and have a
campfire. We can go swimming. Come soon.

         Your friend,
         Max

Monday

1. When are you going to visit your uncle in Reno, Nevada?
2. Did she remember to put sugar in Dad's coffee?
3. what
4. very
5. hunting

Tuesday

1. Snakes, turtles, and alligators all have scales.
2. He doesn't want to read <u>Snow White</u>.
3. Jack's
4. stood
5. feet

Wednesday

1. My friends Carl and Mavis have a new pet rabbit.
2. Why weren't they eating those cookies?
3. gum   gorilla   wiggle
4. b. I saw a dinosaur skeleton in a book.
5. grandmother

Thursday

1. She read <u>Ramona The Pest</u> to Jim and me.
2. We are going fishing Saturday.
3. frog
4. caught
5. A mouse ran across her foot.

Friday

Dear Mrs. Evans,

   Thank you for the toy monkey. It is so soft and cute. I'll take it to bed with me.

                     Your friend,
                     Tonya

Monday

1. My parents were married on June 20, 1989.
2. Do we live on Mars, Earth, or Pluto?
3. drink
4. I
5. story

Tuesday

1. The roses in Dr. Winn's garden bloom in May.
2. What were they doing in the backyard?
3. Easter   Thursday   July
4. <u>2</u>
5. a

Wednesday

1. How big are Walter's feet?
2. Open your umbrella before it begins to rain.
3. Answers will vary.
4. jelly   sheep
5. b. Her chicks came out of the shells.

Thursday

1. Don't play with that sharp knife!
2. Leeza lost four teeth this year.
3. thin
4. taught
5. c. steps to follow when you bake

Friday

Dear Amy,

   Can you come to my house to spend the night? You and I will have fun.

                     Love,
                     Molly

Monday
1. The farmer fed his sheep all winter.
2. When I grow up, I'm going to be a doctor.
3. our
4. we   them   our
5. didn't

Tuesday
1. Were there ants on the picnic table?
2. The carpenter built a tall fence and painted it white.
3. begin
4. women
5. You will need a hammer, nails, paint, and a paintbrush.

Wednesday
1. When did Mr. Ruiz learn to fly an airplane?
2. Do you like <u>Red Riding Hood</u> or <u>Tom Thumb</u>?
3. Answers will vary.
4. blew
5. eat

Thursday
1. He and I went riding Monday morning.
2. What's the small white kitten's name?
3. begging
4. something _2_ Halloween _3_
5. His car was dented.

Friday
1. wasn't
2. It's
3. there
4. quickly
5. smartest

Monday
1. Did you put the milk, butter, and eggs in the refrigerator?
2. Do you want to eat an egg for breakfast?
3. ft.
4. work
5. smiling

Tuesday
1. Those dirty socks stink!
2. Why does Sid have a bigger piece than I have?
   OR Why did Sid get a bigger piece than I?
3. something, rainbow
4. Answers will vary.
5. real

Wednesday
1. Jeff didn't do anything bad.
2. We were laughing at Stan's jokes.
3. tallest
4. older
5. Lara Smith
   217 York Road
   Forest Park, Iowa

Thursday
1. Wasn't that a scary movie?
2. Didn't you go to the Christmas play?
3. drove   stopped
4. He
5. dressed

Friday
1. highest
2. sweeter
3. a   an
4. win
5. won

Monday
1. What did that man ask Annie and her?
2. Did those boys swim in the lake?
3. Mon.
4. a
5. <u>3</u>

Tuesday
1. Roger is my friend. We like to do the same things.
2. What kind of ice cream does she like best?
3. smiling
4. butter   cup
5. Megan opened her umbrella.

Wednesday
1. How do those cats catch mice?
2. Put an apple in the basket.
3. new
4. b. quick with good balance
5. build

Thursday
1. What are you going to do this week?
2. Those dogs rolled in a mud puddle.
3. took
4. Dec.
5. Answers will vary.

Friday
1. men   man
2. He   his
3. me   my
4. don't
5. doesn't

Monday
1. The rooster on Grandpa's farm crows at sunrise.
2. Tim didn't know the way to Dr. Glenn's office.
3. Answers will vary, but must be a number.
4. Pete's
5. rabbits

Tuesday
1. Luis and I picked some oranges in Mr. Lee's orchard.
2. Do Jamal and Tanisha live on Wilson Street?
3. b. ,
4. moose
5. b. money given to the bus driver

Wednesday
1. Ken and I like to play in the snow.
2. Those children skated across an icy pond.
3. Friday
4. b. butterfly   c. Saturday
5. b

Thurdsay
1. Don't put the birdcage on Miss Bell's desk.
2. Are you going to wash the dirty dishes?
3. louder
4. geese
5. a and b

Friday
1. an   a
2. A
3. eat
4. landed
5. swim

Monday
1. Sam and George were best friends.
2. Saturday was so hot that we all went to the beach.
3. need   bead   clean
4. alligator
5. c. July 26, 1995

Tuesday
1. Mr. Feinstein took Sid, David, and Mary to Yellowstone Park.
2. They hate pickles.
3. St.
4. dishes
5. c. Cats have whiskers.

Wednesday
1. Little Bo Peep lost her sheep.
2. A big, black, hairy spider scared Miss Muffet.
3. spoon
4. don't
5. I'll

Thursday
1. Mother was buying shoes for my brother and me.
2. When can Jimmy and I open those Christmas presents?
3. c. a kind of vegetable
4. into
5. merry   happy   glad

Friday
1. foxes
2. geese
3. Mrs.
4. I
5. your

Monday
1. Do they live on Maple Street or West Road?
2. Can you get two sharp pencils for me?
3. some
4. speak, taste
5. coldest

Tuesday
1. Today is May 18, 1997.
2. Did you read <u>Dear Mr. Henshaw</u>?
3. sparkled
4. tree
5. ball   bell   bird   book

Wednesday
1. Mrs. Garcia's little girl was sick.
2. Should she go to see Dr. Hill?
3. last
4. Answers will vary.
5. has

Thursday
1. Don't put that in your mouth!
2. Am I getting presents for my birthday?
3. dived
4. will not
5. a boy named Tony

Friday
1. barked
2. his
3. them
4. have
5. said

Week 31

Monday
1. Why did Manuel run up and down the stairs?
2. Aunt Rosa put chicken, corn, and cookies in a picnic basket.
3. jellyfish
4. c. ran quickly
5. asked

Tuesday
1. Hurray for our team!
2. Martha's hamster ran around on its wheel.
3. buy
4. orange
5. A mouse chewed the wood.

Wednesday
1. Uncle Max eats pancakes, eggs, and bacon every Sunday. OR Uncle Max ate...
2. Clean up that mess right now!
3. fly   tie
4. shipped
5. b and c

Thursday
1. Yoshi didn't do any of his homework.
2. Her pet rabbit had eight babies.
3. story
4. car (OR automobile, truck, bus, etc.)
5. I am

Friday
1. an   a
2. giving
3. can't
4. He   his
5. mopping

Week 32

Monday
1. He and she were taking the dog for a walk.
2. Why didn't you eat the mushrooms on your pizza?
3. happy   shiny   new   big
4. us   her
5. feet   mice

Tuesday
1. How many chickens does Farmer Taylor have?
2. Mr. and Mrs. Morris have four children.
3. helicopter   field   house
4. pond   lake   ocean
5. b. person who brings things

Wednesday
1. My sister and I mowed the lawn on Saturday.
2. Did some flies land on his pudding?
3. bread   butter   jelly   milk
4. inside OR into, applesauce OR pineapple
5. Dear Mr. President,

Thursday
1. Have you read a story about a goose that laid golden eggs?
2. Arnold and Lisa have Mickey Mouse watches.
3. He   it
4. look   see
5. "What is your name?" asked Anita.

Friday
1. a. apostrophe   b. period   c. period
2. a. apostrophe   b. apostrophe   c. question mark
3. a. apostrophe   b. comma   c. period

Week 33

Monday
1. Mr. Clark is a vet at the San Diego Zoo.
2. You'd better hurry. The school bus is coming.
3. Answers will vary.
4. Let's
5. sing

Tuesday
1. I have some cupcakes. Do you want one?
2. An old man sat on the bench and ate an apple.
3. over
4. then
5. I make funny faces.

Wednesday
1. I can't play now. Can you come back later?
2. Ringling Brothers Circus is coming to town on October 19.
3. Annie said, "I like chocolate ice cream."
4. peaches
5. know

Thursday
1. Let's plant flowers by Mrs. Olson's fence.
2. My room is a mess. Mom says I have to clean it now.
3. jump
4. goat   horse   pig   sheep
5. friend

Friday
1. a. yes   b. no   c. yes
2. a. no   b. yes   c. yes
3. a. yes   b. yes   c. no

        Daily Language Review, Grade 2 • EMC 580 • ©2005 Evan-Moor Corp.